INTRODUCTION

UNIT 1 DRAWING   11

EILEEN ADAMS

Introduction

Session 1: Near and far

Session 2: Backdrop

Session 3: In action

Session 4: Touching textures

Session 5: Contrasting combinations

Other areas of learning

UNIT 2 PAINTING   23

JUDY GRAHAME

Introduction

Session 1: What is a still life?

Session 2: Creating a composition

Session 3: Colour and tone

Session 4: The effects of colour

Session 5: From another viewpoint

Other areas of learning

UNIT 3 PRINTING   35

MICHÈLE CLAIRE KITTO

Introduction

Session 1: Exploring pattern –
the Victorian designers

Session 2: Designing a motif for a pattern

Session 3: Printing designs by hand

Session 4: Printing using a photocopier

Session 5: Selecting a final design

Other areas of learning

UNIT 4 TEXTILES   47

JANE BOWER

Introduction

Session 1: Felting

Session 2: Fabric manipulation – circles

Session 3: Weaving on card looms

Session 4: Batik

Session 5: Quilted batik

Other areas of learning

UNIT 5 SCULPTURE   59

ROSEMARY BIGNELL

Introduction

Session 1: The figure in motion

Session 2: Techniques using wire

Session 3: Constructing an armature

Session 4: Modelling form

Session 5: Painting figures, reviewing
and evaluating

Other areas of learning

UNIT 6 DIGITAL MEDIA   71

KEVIN MATHIESON

Introduction

Session 1: Self-image

Session 2: Making and completing
the structure

Session 3: Victorian paper costumes

Session 4: Character stories and costumes

Session 5: Creating the character story

Other areas of learning

ABOUT ART EXPRESS

Art Express was developed at a time of change. It builds upon the first national curriculum which established the underlying principles, content and practice of art education. However, it allows schools to take ownership of their own curriculum content and to tailor it for their specific needs. *Art Express* illustrates how high-quality subject teaching can still be used to underwrite the development and evolution of new curriculum practice and supports teachers' professional development. Core to this approach are the role of new media, the significance of cross-curricular areas of learning and the importance of drawing as a key element of learning. The series covers the primary concepts and key processes of art education via six content areas –

- ■ Drawing
- ■ Painting
- ■ Printing
- ■ Textiles
- ■ Sculpture
- ■ Digital Media

Philosophy

Art Express is underwritten by clear principles about the nature and role of art in education. Central to this lies the understanding of art education as a process of generating ideas, realising them in material form, and being able to talk about what was done and why. This is best expressed as a set of three principles underlying each unit and session. They are seen clearly in the consistent pattern of learning objectives and assessment outcomes. Such principles are not unique to art education, and teachers will recognise the broader areas of learning and the duties of the school to prepare pupils for the experiences of later life.
The three principles are related to:
- ■ The development of ideas and creativity
- ■ The development of skills and mastery of processes
- ■ The development of knowledge encompassing art and cultures.

Art and Education

Art Express takes a broad view of education and the role that art can play. Its principles echo across the curriculum. They indicate how art can contribute to essential aspects of children's personal development such as creativity, independence, judgement and self-reflection.

Art Express includes regular opportunities to learn about and explore other cultures: celebrating different cultural traditions while avoiding outdated stereotypes that should no longer have a place in children's understanding of our multicultural world.

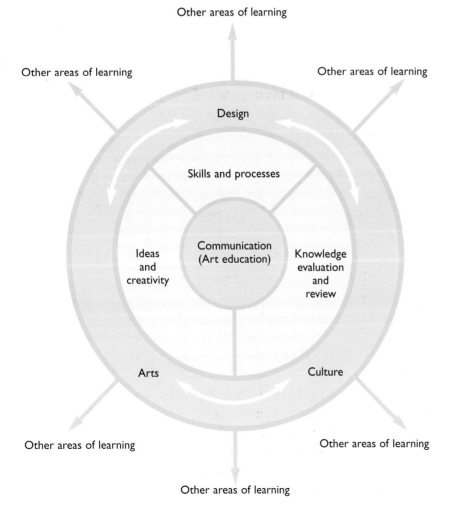

IN THE CLASSROOM

Teaching

The units in *Art Express* exemplify good practice in teaching. They are written to model progression from first-hand experimentation and the acquisition of skills and technical knowledge, towards applying what has been learned with new independence and purpose, enabling children to become self-aware as well as confident learners.

Planning

The *Art Express* units have sequential logic and may be used as a scheme of work. The units build upon prior learning – progression and continuity are built into the scheme. The programme for each year ensures that the breadth and balance of experience, skills and curriculum content is appropriate for the age range.

However, from the outset, the editorial board of *Art Express* have been anxious to create a model of practice that is open to change and modification by creative teachers. Teachers will find it easy to adapt units to fit in with local circumstances and curriculum. For instance, all units may be adapted for different age ranges, purposes and contexts.

In *Art Express*, the units illustrate how planned learning is sequential and cumulative. They model the process of enquiry and experimentation that generates ideas and develops familiarity with materials. This then generates purposeful ideas and plans, following these through, mastering skills and reviewing progress.

Each unit contains a sequence of sessions. These are not necessarily lessons of a fixed length but separate learning segments. For instance, some of the sessions in the Digital Media units are a series of short episodes, each of which must be completed before moving on. Teachers can manage these in different ways – for example, by using small groups or by adapting material from one session to cover several weeks. Alternatively, an arts week could compress sessions within a short time-frame, possibly held across the school, with activities for each year group structured from their appropriate book.

Assessment

Art Express provides a good model for assessment of learning. It offers examples of what teachers should observe pupils do, to confirm that they have made anticipated gains in learning. Units often plan explicitly for children to discuss their findings, especially via the plenary. This offers the opportunity to assess children's comprehension and to review the next steps. It also reinforces the expectation for pupils to become partners in the assessment of their own progress, and thus become more independent learners.

Art Express supports the increasing emphasis upon personalised learning by giving practical suggestions for managing issues such as differentiation in addition to reflection opportunities and self-assessment rubrics.

WHAT'S IN THE BOOKS

Below
Each unit has an introduction page with key issues and aims for the topic.

Bottom left and right
Double-page spreads follow, with instructions for carrying out each session, including learning objectives and assessment for learning. Images on session pages show examples of work from pupils who have trialled each project.

Right
Other areas of learning offers ideas for extending the topic across the curriculum.

UNITS

The units in *Art Express* illustrate teaching and learning within six areas of experience – Painting, Printing, Sculpture, Textiles, Drawing and Digital Media. The first four units support learning through the progressive development of experience, skills and knowledge.

Drawing is seen as a key skill that underwrites all activity in art, and most units include it as ideas and plans are developed and revised. The Drawing units themselves provide a complementary approach and can often be used in conjunction with other units. As stand-alone units, they focus on drawing as a means of perception, invention and communication and involve drawing from observation, memory and imagination.

Similarly, the Digital Media units have a dual role, in that the techniques and processes can be adapted and incorporated directly into the other units as part of exploring and developing ideas. Most of the Digital Media units seek to engage pupils directly with some first-hand experience of materials, and outcomes are often a combination of digital plus practical skills and techniques and demonstrate how digital media may be used creatively to support learning through art.

The units of work have been developed to support good practice in planning and assessment and in challenging children to reach high standards and to use their creativity and imagination. They also provide clear and practical advice and guidance on teaching the skills and techniques that pupils will need to master in order to achieve success.

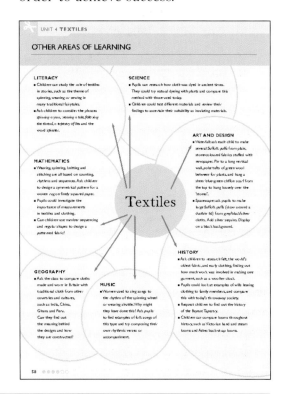

WHAT'S ON THE CD-ROM

The following supporting materials are available on the CD-ROM:

- Resource sheets – photocopiable and whiteboard resources for pupils and teachers
- Teacher assessment sheet per unit
- Pupil self-evaluation sheet per unit
- *PowerPoint* presentations
- Image library of Artists' works
- Library of reference images
- Image library of Children's work from trial schools
- Virtual gallery with specially commissioned software to allow uploading of pupils' work
- Teachers reference including 'Skills and Processes' chart, list of suppliers and session-by-session unit vocabulary.

RESOURCES

Art Express provides a range of additional resources for teachers and pupils on the complementary CD-ROM. Teachers will find these resources inspire and illuminate learning by presenting exciting visual examples and references. These resources are starting-points, examples and signposts – teachers will find many more resources locally and will adapt these to expand the collection.

Viewing art on screen from disks or the internet brings opportunities to

see many large, bright images of art, craft and design. Wherever possible, teachers should also lead their pupils to first-hand or hands-on experience of real arts, bringing artefacts into the classroom and organising outings to local art galleries and museums.

Finally, the CD-ROM contains an interactive **Virtual Gallery** – specially created software that will enable pupils to build their own art galleries to support reflection and discussion, and to celebrate the individual work of the school.

Above and left
Image library, including images of children's work.

Left
PowerPoint presentations include information and demonstrations for teachers and pupils.

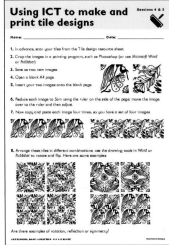

Far left and centre
Photocopiable and whiteboard resources for pupils and teachers.

Left
Pupil self-evaluation and teacher assessment sheets support each unit.

HOW TO USE THE CD-ROM

GETTING STARTED

- **PC**: the *Art Express* programme should auto-run when you insert the CD-ROM. If not, use My Computer to browse the contents of the CD-ROM and click on the File setup.
- **Mac**: insert the CD-ROM and double-click the *Art Express* icon. Open the folder and double-click the *Art Express* icon inside.

NETWORKING

Schools that have purchased a site licence are permitted to install and save the CD-Rom on a server and allow access on workstations within the school. Out-of-school access is not permitted, and image download permissions remain as above.

Use the MSI installer to deploy *Art Express* if you have a suitable network, or install *Art Express* to a server using the method described in Getting Started. Then, at each workstation, browse to the Installation folder on the server and run the File setup. Follow the instructions to create a shortcut to *Art Express* on the workstation.

TECHNICAL SUPPORT

Email A&C Black Customer Services on educationalsales@acblack.com.

MINIMUM SPECIFICATION

- PC with CD-ROM drive: Windows 98, 2000, XP or Vista
- Processor: Pentium 2 (or equivalent), 1GHz
- Ram: 256 MB
- Graphics: 800 x 600, 16-bit display, 3D accelerator (recommended)
- Mac with CD-ROM drive: OS X 10.1.5 and above
- Processor: G4 1GHz
- Ram: 256 MB
- Graphics: 800 x 600, 16-bit display,
- 3D accelerator (recommended)

CD-ROM NAVIGATION

Main menu

From the main menu, teachers can access each of the following areas of the CD:

1. Teacher Resources

Access the bank of artist's and children's work, photos and videos, plus PDF and *PowerPoint* resources. Also view the artwork that you import from other sources.

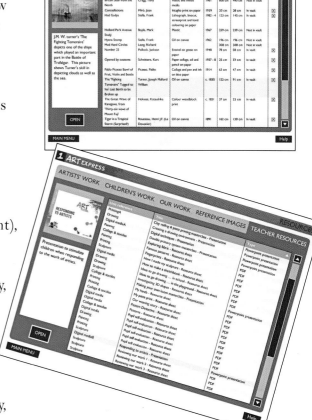

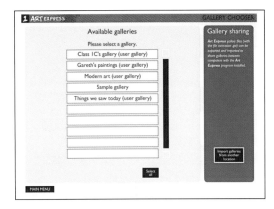

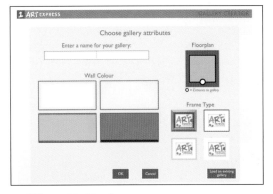

2. View Galleries
View the default virtual 3D galleries, together with the ones that you create. In this book there is only one pre-set gallery.

3. Create a Gallery
Use this to create your own virtual 3D gallery. Choose your floorplan, wall colour and framing theme, then get artist's work from the vault – or your own imported artwork – and position the pieces on the walls.

4. Our work
Use this to import image files into the programme to use in a virtual gallery or transfer them to another computer with *Art Express* installed.

1. Teacher Resources Menu
Once in the Teacher Resources menu, the following resources are accessed:

a) Images
There are three types of images available on the CD-ROM:

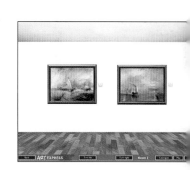

■ **Image library of Artists' work**
These are specific images referred to in the sessions; some may be imported into the **Virtual Gallery**, but not all.
Note: None of these images can be printed due to copyright provisions.

■ **Library of reference images**
These are additional images, which may be referred to during sessions, or be used for reference or stimulus.

■ **Image library of Children's work**
These are images of work created by children during the trialling of the units in schools.

b) Resource sheets
Photocopiable and whiteboard resources for pupils and teachers.

c) Assessment sheets
Pupil self-evaluation and teacher assessment sheets support each unit.

d) Presentations
PowerPoint presentations for teachers and pupils, as well as masterclasses for teachers, which can be shared with pupils. (To alter or adapt the *PowerPoint* files, use these files stored in the folder on the CD-ROM.)

e) Teachers' planning
Includes a 'Skills and Processes' chart for longterm planning, a list of suppliers and session-by-session vocabulary for each unit.

DRAWING IS DIFFERENT

Art Express supports contemporary curriculum modelling and planning as well as providing detailed guidance and support for teaching. The units of work have been developed to support good practice in planning, assessment and challenging pupils to reach high standards and to use their creativity and imagination. They also provide clear and practical guidance on teaching the skills and techniques that children will need to master in order to achieve success.

Foundation skill

In *Art Express*, drawing is seen as a core skill that underpins all activity in art. Indeed, as ideas and plans are developed and revised, most units will indicate the significant role of drawing via perception, invention and communication.

The Drawing units themselves bear witness to the philosophy that sees the production of drawing as an internal dialogue for making choices, judgements and decisions – via observation, memory and imagination. The development of this internal communication strategy runs through every activity and each unit.

Technique and development

In learning to draw, pupils will gain experience of a wide range of tools and materials. They will develop a range of strategies and learn how drawing can be used for different purposes. However, teachers are invited to see drawing not purely as a set of techniques, but as a process that has much to do with attitude, habit, the ability to make connections and, above all, to be creative.

Expert author

The Drawing units have been written by Eileen Adams who directs *Power Drawing*, the professional development programme of The Campaign for Drawing. This publishes numerous books on the role of drawing as an essential and intrinsic part of learning and as a strategy for thinking.

Cross-curricular application

The Drawing units are presented in a similar way to the other units, but teachers should use the activities and techniques as means of enriching and extending thinking and learning – across the curriculum, wherever pupils are invited to think, look, speculate, imagine and come up with fresh ideas.

These activities are presented for use with particular age ranges and can be followed sequentially to provide a rich and intensive experience of drawing. Creative teachers, however, will also see opportunities to use these ideas for lessons in other sequences, with other age ranges and in a variety of curriculum situations.

For more information about The Campaign for Drawing and the work of Eileen Adams, go to www.campaignfordrawing.org/education/index.aspx

Drawing is not only about making marks on paper to represent things: it is about understanding experience and ideas, and sharing that knowledge. It is about making meaning. Pupils draw to explore their world, to understand it and to communicate their ideas to others. Drawing prompts a personal and emotional response. It can also be a shared activity, providing a means for interaction and collaboration.

Prior to Year 6, children will have had exposure to using drawing to reflect on their experience and to rework it, so that they understand it. They should have a clear idea of the range of purposes for which they use drawing, and be able to choose appropriate drawing strategies and techniques.

The drawing units in *Arts Express* focus on learning through drawing using five themes: place, nature, buildings, people and things in the wider environment. The unit in this book includes a range of drawing techniques: memory map, pictorial map, large-scale map, flick book, simple animation, *scrafitto*, blind drawings and pattern-making.

It encourages children to work with drawing in these different ways to increase their awareness of their physical and social environment; to help them reflect on familiar surroundings; and to encourage a personal and emotional response to the built and natural environment, and to people and things.

It develops observational, analytical and organisational skills, as well as skills of interpretation and invention.

It introduces a range of drawing techniques, extends children's visual and verbal vocabulary and develops their social skills and ability to collaborate with others, extending their powers of reason and facilitating discussion and sharing of ideas.

AIMS

This unit offers pupils the opportunity to:

- collect and share ideas, and explore and experiment with materials
- use a range of drawing strategies and techniques
- understand that marks can have meanings
- develop control over a variety of drawing tools and materials, using them selectively and purposefully.
- look at different kinds of drawings, talk about them and try to interpret them.

ASSESSMENT FOR LEARNING

Assessment should focus not only on how well children can draw, but also on what each child learns through drawing. This will include:

Knowledge: of people and place, self and others, the natural and the made world.

Skills: of observation, analysis, interpretation, imagination, invention, expression and communication.

Attitudes: confidence to engage in drawing activities, willingness to experiment and be playful and capacity to deal with failure and frustration positively and creatively, preparedness to the reflective and eagerness to communicate.

By the end of this unit, can children understand their experiences better, as well as shape their ideas and communicate more effectively through the medium of drawing?

> ▶ **CD-ROM RESOURCES**
> - Presentation: Developing drawing
> - Images and artworks
> - Resource sheets:
>   - Questions to ask when looking at a map
>   - Ideas to go drawing… Place
>   - More ideas to go drawing
> - Teacher assessment
> - Pupil self-evaluation

SESSION I **PLACE: NEAR AND FAR**

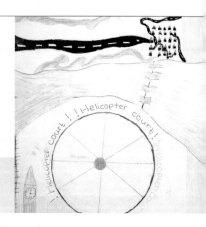

LEARNING OBJECTIVES

Children will:

- learn more about how art can construct and communicate meaning by reading and interpreting different kinds of map
- learn to make and use symbols by creating maps

- develop further social skills of communication, negotiation and collaboration.

VOCABULARY map, local, region, symbol, scale, feature, zoom in, zoom out, bird's-eye view

▼ **RESOURCES**

- different kinds of map, for example: pictorial, tourist maps, OS maps, A–Z maps (Note: always check copyright permission issues, particularly if using copies of maps)
- internet access to view maps, for example: Google maps, Multimap, street maps
- A1 and A2 paper
- felt-tip pens and markers (assorted colours)
- resource sheet: Questions to ask when looking at a map; Ideas to go drawing… Place

▼ **ASSESSMENT FOR LEARNING**

Can the children:

- recognise different types of convention used in map-making?
- identify and interpret symbols used on maps?
- create their own symbols and maps?

ACTIVITY

In this session, pupils will look at different kinds of map, then work together in groups to create three maps for a display.

- Use the internet and the interactive whiteboard to demonstrate different ways of viewing the school – bird's-eye view, aerial view, OS map and street map. Ask the children to discuss with a partner what they can see.
- Provide pupils with resources – atlases, internet access and maps – to explore different kinds of map. Ask them to focus on maps of the local area, the nearest town and the wider region. Invite small groups to discuss the idea of scale and compare the scales on the different maps they are using. Provide a list of questions for the children to use when looking at the maps, or use the **Questions to ask when looking at a map** resource sheet.
- Next, explain that they will create three kinds of map: the local area, the town and the region.

LOCAL AREA

This is a memory map that pupils construct from their knowledge of the immediate area around the school. Their familiarity will depend on how close they live to the school and whether they come on foot or by car. Pupils can check how accurate their memory is when they compare their map with the bird's-eye view and street maps on the internet. This can be part of a class discussion – you could select internet-based maps to show on the interactive whiteboard.

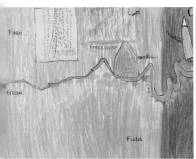

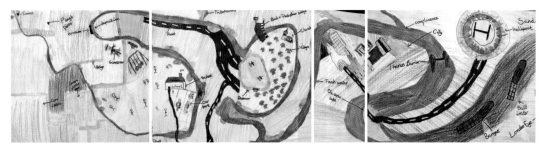

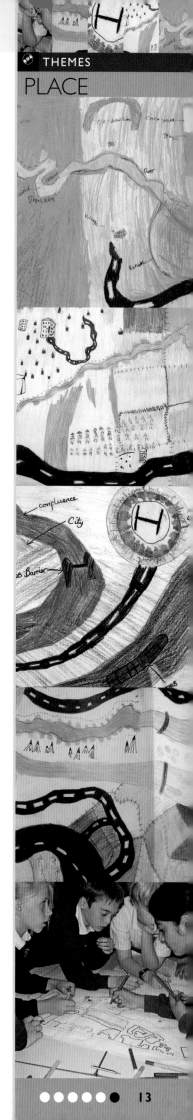

TOWN MAP

This is a pictorial map, developed in small groups. Invite pupils to contribute suggestions about what should be included – important buildings, shops, parks and open spaces. Ask them to use an internet map or an atlas to locate the position of main roads, railways, rivers or other landmarks. They can then make and arrange drawings of the key elements in the town in appropriate places to build up an interesting collaged picture. When complete, ask the groups to compare their maps and discuss how each group chose to portray the town.

REGIONAL MAP

Ask the whole class, working in small groups, to interpret sections of an OS map of the region. Use the computer and interactive whiteboard to zoom in and out of the wider region to help pupils identify key features and discuss how a map is constructed using symbols. Challenge the children to build up their own version of the map

in sections. Members of each group will have to negotiate how their sections of the map will connect with that of the next group, so key features such as rivers and roads should be put in place first. Pupils need to agree what symbols and conventions they will use to create their maps (they could create their own).

■ When completed, the children can join up the sections to create one large map. Focus discussion on the different conventions and symbols that have been used. Ask the groups to discuss the process of making their maps. Why do we need these maps and how do we use them? Ask them to talk about the merits of the different kinds of map they have investigated and the strengths and weaknesses of each. Each group could write an appraisal of their process, which could be attached to the display, or make a sound recording for others to listen to.

■ Pupils could undertake further drawing tasks, such as those suggested in the **Ideas to go drawing… Place** resource sheet.

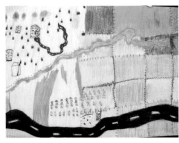

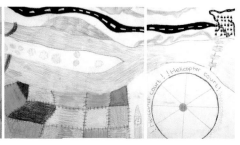

DIFFERENTIATION

Children who have not progressed as far…
These pupils can make drawings to compare OS symbols with those of their own design.

Children who have progressed further…
Pupils who are confident in reading, interpreting and making maps can create a map of their own of a fantasy environment.

SESSION 2 **BUILDINGS: BACKDROP**

LEARNING OBJECTIVES

Children will:

- extend and refine their technical skills
- extend their ability to design and create purposefully by learning a simple animation technique
- further develop their ability to communicate meaning by constructing a narrative visually and verbally.

VOCABULARY action, animation, backdrop, background, frame, movement, narrative, pin-figure, position, sequence, template

▼ RESOURCES

- ▶ A4 paper
- ▶ scissors
- ▶ stapler
- ▶ assorted drawing tools and media
- ▶ video camera, *Digital Blue* camera or webcam (optional)
- ▶ A2 paper
- ▶ lining paper
- ▶ sugar paper, assorted colours
- ▶ card scraps, assorted colours
- ▶ adhesive
- ▶ split pins to secure body parts of the figure
- ▶ digital camera
- ▶ resource sheet: More ideas to go drawing

▼ ASSESSMENT FOR LEARNING

Can the children:
- ▶ draw from memory and imagination?
- ▶ visualise and present a narrative sequence?
- ▶ make a flick book?

ACTIVITY

In this session, pupils will discuss ideas about expressing movement through drawing.

■ Explore the idea of a flick book: a series of pictures that vary from page to page so that when the pages are turned quickly, the sequence creates an impression of movement.

■ Ask the children to create their own flick book by folding and cutting a piece of A4 paper into 16 small pages, and stapling them (make thicker books using a bulldog clip). Challenge pupils to make a series of drawings on the pages to illustrate a simple movement, such as a falling stick, a bouncing ball, or a person moving. Encourage them to discuss how one drawing relates to the next and how a sense of movement is suggested by the way the marks are made and positioned. If you have access to a video camera, *Digital Blue* camera or webcam, record the children doing simple tasks, replay the recording frame by frame, then ask pupils to create drawings in place of the recorded frames.

■ Initiate a discussion about how buildings create a backdrop to much of human activity. Ask the children to think about their journey to school, the features they notice and what they see happening. Are there public, commercial or residential buildings? Are there any open spaces? Are people walking, or waiting at bus stops? Are they working or window-shopping? Invite pupils to make quick mental maps to remind them of key features and landmarks. If these drawings are done on A2 paper, with a zigzag line to denote the route, everything will fit in.

■ Working in groups of four, ask pupils to compare their maps and discuss their favourite part of the journey. Then invite them to select key features from each of their maps to plan a combined group townscape.

■ Ask the children to use sugar paper and paper scraps on lining paper to construct a townscape collage that will

act as a backdrop for an animation of a moving figure. Each group member is responsible for part of the backdrop – pupils will have to agree not only on the elements to be included, but also on scale, colour scheme and the arrangement in order to create a coherent townscape.

■ Ask each child to create a figure with movable parts: head and neck, torso, upper and lower arms, hands, thighs, lower legs and feet. Join the parts with split pins to create a figure capable of being manipulated. The clothes of the figure should hint at the character being portrayed. Is it a male or a female? A real or fictitious person? Does it wear distinctive dress or uniform, such as a clown, an athlete or perhaps a police officer?

■ The children can take turns, placing their figure on the backdrop, moving it along little by little, and remembering to move the limbs to new positions to suggest that the figure is moving. At each position, take a single frame photograph using a digital camera. A flick book can be made from the thumbnails or small prints of the images. Alternatively, the sequence of images could be used to create an animation, using *Flash* or similar.

■ Ask pupils to discuss what they learned with a 'talking partner', and then feed back to the class. Everyone should participate in the discussion.

■ Further drawing tasks are available on the **More ideas to go drawing** resource sheet.

DIFFERENTIATION

Children who have not progressed as far…
These pupils can make more jointed figures to create groups of action figures. They could focus on more specific flick books or animated sequences with a digital camera for display or presentation.

Children who have progressed further…
These pupils can create another flick book that tells a story without words. They could recreate effects similar to those of a paper-based flick book using a programme such as *Windows Movie Maker* to build their sequence of images into an animation.

SESSION 3 **PEOPLE: IN ACTION**

LEARNING OBJECTIVES

Children will:

- refine their technical skills and develop their ability to observe, record and appreciate qualities of movement and gesture

- develop further knowledge and understanding of different techniques.

VOCABULARY **action, balance, direction, dynamic, imbalance, movement, poised, transition, viewpoint, weight**

▼ RESOURCES

- sketchbooks
- fibre-tip pens
- ballpoint pens
- black marker pens
- charcoal
- digital cameras
- video camera (optional)
- illustrations from newspapers and magazines
- internet access
- CD-ROM: images of athletes and dancers
- resource sheet: More ideas to go drawing

▼ ASSESSMENT FOR LEARNING

Can the children:
- infuse drawings with energy and dynamism?
- use a variety of techniques to explore the idea of human movement?

ACTIVITY

In this session, pupils will focus on drawing figures in motion. See the Sculpture unit in this book for more on this topic.

■ Ask the children to use one of their breaks or part of a lunch time to record in their sketchbooks various examples of pupils moving in the playground. Ask them to observe carefully, but to draw quickly to record the sense of movement. To help them do this, suggest they observe certain things. Is the child upright or leaning forward? Are they balanced on one foot? Where are the other leg and foot? Are the knees bent? Where are the arms? The drawings do not have to look much like figures. They may look more like diagrams. They are not drawings of people so much as note-taking about movement.

■ Ask the children to work in pairs. One child runs in slow motion and the other observes this and draws a series of stick figures to show the position of torso, head, arms and legs. Then ask the two to change places and repeat the activity. If available, pupils could use a digital or video camera to help with this task.

■ In a PE lesson in the playground or hall, invite the children to run, jump, skip and hop. When you blow a whistle, they freeze. Repeat the exercise with pupils moving to music. When the whistle blows or the music is stopped, the children must stay in their positions. Ask pupils to get into

pairs. If available, give a digital camera to one of each pair to photograph the movements of their partner before and during the pauses. After a set period of time they swap, and the other child works the camera. This will create a collection of images that the children can refer to later.

■ Encourage pupils to collect images of sportsmen and women, athletes and dancers from newspapers, magazines and the internet (some are also available on the CD-ROM). These will create another bank of images for the class to use. A display of images can prompt a useful discussion about movement, bringing into play the vocabulary that will inform their drawing – particularly ideas related to weight and balance.

■ The children now have a selection of photographs to work from, as well as their memories of the sensation of moving plus sketches from observing motion. Ask pupils to choose

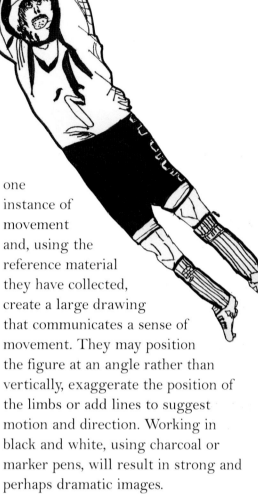

one instance of movement and, using the reference material they have collected, create a large drawing that communicates a sense of movement. They may position the figure at an angle rather than vertically, exaggerate the position of the limbs or add lines to suggest motion and direction. Working in black and white, using charcoal or marker pens, will result in strong and perhaps dramatic images.

■ Place the drawings on display and invite pupils to choose which one (not their own) they think conveys the sense of movement effectively. Challenge them to explain how it achieves this. Ask questions, such as: *Whose drawing shows human movement really well? Why? What could they do to improve their drawing further?* Everyone should be encouraged to participate in the discussion.

■ Additional drawing tasks and suggestions are available on the **More ideas to go drawing** resource sheet.

DIFFERENTIATION

Children who have not progressed as far...
These pupils should experiment further until they are able to draw movement, both from observation and from photographs.

Children who have progressed further...
Pupils who are confident drawing movement should make copies on acetate of some of their sketches, then project these using an overhead projector to build up a drawing of a group of figures moving.

SESSION 4 **NATURE: TOUCHING TEXTURES**

LEARNING OBJECTIVES
Children will:

- learn to observe and confidently record the quality of surfaces and textures

- enrich and refine their understanding of techniques and use of materials by exploring and recording tonal qualities
- develop skills of interpretation.

VOCABULARY contrast, impression, layered, resist, scraffito, scraperboard, spirit, texture, tonal, tone

▼ RESOURCES

▶ sketchbooks
▶ pens
▶ digital camera
▶ assorted papers
▶ wax crayon
▶ scraperboard
▶ chalk
▶ charcoal
▶ candles
▶ soft pencils
▶ graphite
▶ watercolours
▶ inks

▼ ASSESSMENT FOR LEARNING

Can the children:
▶ draw in a spontaneous way?
▶ use a variety of techniques to explore and represent tonal qualities, selecting and using materials and tools appropriately?
▶ show in their drawing, conversation and writing that they can appreciate and distinguish different aesthetic qualities?

ACTIVITY

In this session, pupils will explore texture in natural forms.

- Take the children for a walk to observe and collect natural forms. While on their walk, suggest they make quick sketches in their sketchbooks of clumps of grass, twigs, stones and plants, recording impressions of nature around them. Invite them to collect things that have an interesting texture (not living plant material). Pupils can also take photographs to refer to back in the classroom.

- In class, offer the children a variety of tools and materials to experiment with creating textures.

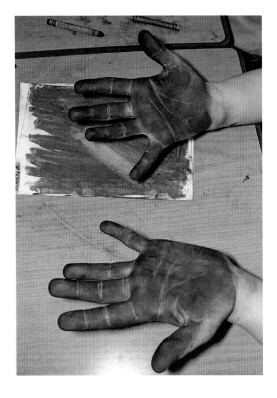

Encourage them to:

- work both very quickly and very slowly
- try working with dots, splashes and splodges, as well as lines and shapes
- try overlaying colours with wax crayons, and scraping away parts of the surface
- work with hatching and cross-hatching on scraperboard
- work on rough paper and rub in chalk and charcoal with the fingers or the hand
- mix soft pencil and ink
- try any other combinations of media that create a range of tones.

This is an opportunity to bring into play many of the techniques the children have previously learned. Put these experimental drawings to one side for a class discussion later.

- Ask pupils to handle the material they found outdoors and try to describe what it feels like. (This can be made more vivid if the child puts their hands behind their back and someone passes them the object.) Ask them to view the tones and textures they created through their experiments on paper, and choose any that seem to echo the textural qualities they found in the physical objects.

- Ask the children to work in pairs and take turns at this activity. Again, one child feels an object behind their back

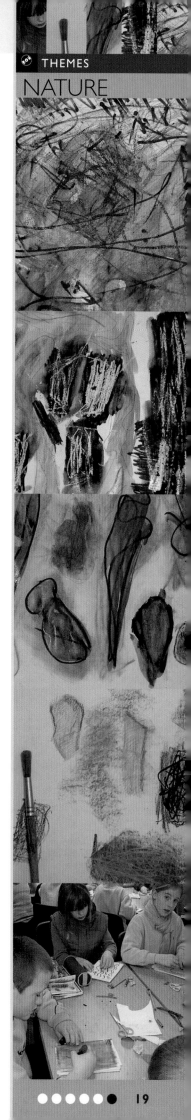

and tries to describe the sensations experienced in handling the natural form; the other responds to the description through drawing. Pupils might describe an object verbally as *rough, smooth, woody, woolly, prickly, soft* or *crumbly.* They might say *it has ridges and hollows, or a jagged edge.* They might describe it as *cool to the touch.* The person drawing has to interpret these qualities through the marks made on the paper, selecting from the media and techniques they experimented with previously. If the children work on A1 paper, they can be encouraged to make large gestural drawings, with broad sweeps of the arm, rather than small, neat, careful, drawings. If there is time, they could add some drawings from observation.

■ Display the children's texture drawings together with the objects. Ask them to write words on sticky notes that they think describe the surface quality of their objects, and place these on the display. Then ask them to write, on a different coloured sticky note, what each drawing reminds them of or suggests to them and stick these on too. These prompts could lead to the creation of an imaginative drawing or poem.

■ Gather the class to discuss the work on display and the texture experiments from the start of the session. Ask questions, such as: *Which drawings show the textures of the objects really well? Can you recognise what natural forms any of the experimental drawings were based on?*

DIFFERENTIATION

Children who have not progressed as far...
These pupils should experiment further to create a number of textured surfaces, and then superimpose outline shapes of natural forms drawn from observation.

Children who have progressed further...
These pupils could try doing 'blind' drawings. They choose an object, which they feel with one hand and draw with the other hand. However, they are blindfolded, so they can see neither the object nor the drawing. The children can work in pairs and guide each other.

SESSION 5 THINGS: CONTRASTING COMBINATIONS

LEARNING OBJECTIVES
Children will:
- further develop and refine skills and techniques
- develop greater confidence in creating images and experimenting with ideas
- learn to recognise and appreciate contrasting qualities and to evaluate their own and others' work.

VOCABULARY geometric, organic, regular, irregular, freeform, accidental, complementary, contrast, deliberate, pattern, random, regular, relation, repetition, spontaneous

▼ RESOURCES

- ▶ variety of drawing tools
- ▶ range of drawing materials
- ▶ selection of papers
- ▶ drawings by artists and designers that show the use of pattern
- ▶ pupil self-evaluation sheet

▼ ASSESSMENT FOR LEARNING

Can the children:
- ▶ select and use materials and tools appropriately, and combine a variety of techniques purposefully to develop a drawing?
- ▶ take steps to improve their work, including making positive use of accidents and mistakes?
- ▶ talk with confidence and perception about the qualities to be found in their own work and that of artists they have studied?

ACTIVITY

In this session, pupils will look at contrast and pattern.

■ Invite the children to think about the shapes, colours and patterns they encounter in everyday objects and discuss how shapes might be described, for example: *geometric, organic, regular, irregular, freeform*. Which things are patterned and which are plain? Which colours work in harmony and which

are contrasting? What makes a pattern? Ask pupils to name items that could show regular repetition of shape, such as mugs on a shelf, birds on a wire or beads on a string.

■ Ask pupils to work in pairs to find examples of contrasting shapes, patterns and colours in the classroom. These could be a bright, shiny book placed on soft fabric; a delicately coloured and patterned shell set on top of brightly coloured card; or a piece of string dropped randomly on a checked duster. Ask the pairs to show their contrasts to the class, explaining their selections. If possible, some of these should be retained to make a small display, so the children have a reminder of the nature of contrasts. Alternatively, take digital photographs to create a photographic exhibition.

■ Explain to the class that they are going to draw in two very different ways: deliberately and carefully, then spontaneously and experimentally.

■ First ask the children to draw one of the objects from the initial activity from observation. They can use any tools or materials, but they should concentrate on shape, form and pattern or surface decoration, be very deliberate about the marks they make and try to be as accurate as possible.

■ The second drawing should be done in a very free way, experimenting with ways of making marks: dribbling,

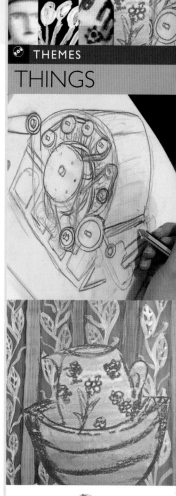

splattering and blowing coloured inks; trying to capture shadows of leaves blowing in the breeze; connecting random marks; or perhaps repeating rhythmic lines superimposed on each other.

■ When pupils have completed both drawings, ask them to do a third, using elements from the previous two drawings – the object from the first drawing and ideas for the background from the experimental mark making. The aim is to put them together to create a composition of a patterned object on a patterned background. Encourage the children to be bold with their use of colour. They may wish to draw with wax resist and coloured inks, with paint or use cut-outs of coloured paper to which pattern is applied.

■ The class might look at drawings by Matisse and consider how he used colour and pattern – as background, to suggest forms or as contrasts.

■ Put all the drawings on display in their groups of three and invite pupils to give their final piece a title. Ask them to discuss the different ways they have answered the brief.

■ Which drawings are good examples of contrast? Why?
■ Which are examples of interesting ways to create patterns?
■ Which have successful colour combinations? Why?
■ Which drawings are bold and lively?
■ Which drawings are more delicate and subtle?
■ Which is their favourite drawing (not their own)? Why?
■ What could they do to improve their own drawing?
■ How might they use art in future, in their personal lives or at school?

■ At the end of the session, provide each child with the **Pupil self-evaluation** sheet for feedback on the work undertaken in the unit.

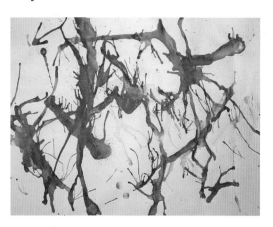

DIFFERENTIATION

Children who have not progressed as far...
These pupils should experiment further so they are able to find ways to create different kinds of pattern.

Children who have progressed further...
These pupils could use photographs as a reference to create a poster based on a composition of overlapping animals. This should make use of the different markings on the animals to emphasise the use of pattern.

OTHER AREAS OF LEARNING

LITERACY

■ Ask pupils to choose one of their favourite books to make into a film or a play. Invite them to draw what the characters would look like and design costumes for them.

■ Create a movement vocabulary bank – encourage the children to create a word-bank of movement words, which they can illustrate. They could use the words and drawings to make a book, or scan the drawings and use a computer to combine them with the words.

GEOGRAPHY

■ How do pupils come to school? Do they walk, or travel by bus or by car? How would they improve parking for the school? Ask the children to draw up a plan to show how car parking could be changed both outside the school and inside the school grounds to create a safer and better quality environment.

SCIENCE

■ Ask the children to make a diagram or a series of drawings to show how a plant or animal grows or develops.

MATHEMATICS

■ Ask pupils to make a drawing of a leaf on a grid. Then ask them to make another drawing with the scale increased by 100%. Can they make a new drawing where they decrease the scale of this by 50%?

Drawing

SCIENCE

■ Can pupils draw a container that they would find in nature (for example, a fruit, seed pod, beehive, bird's nest, or crab shell)? Using nature as inspiration, invite the children to design a container for food, things or people. They should annotate their drawings to show the connections with the natural world.

HISTORY

■ Challenge pupils to imagine they live in another century. Which historical period would they choose? Encourage them to find out about the clothes they and their family would wear. Ask them to draw a family gathering – a wedding or a party – where people would wear their best clothes and accessories.

■ Ask the children to add furniture and décor, as well as food and drink to their drawing.

ICT

■ Pupils could make a computer animation of a moving figure using video or digital photographs and *Windows Movie Maker* or *PowerPoint*.

■ Children could scan natural objects into the computer using a visualiser or digital camera and then add scans of different textures as layers.

Painting provides a wonderful arena in which pupils can immerse themselves in the world of colour. As one of the fundamental processes within art and design, children should be provided with copious opportunities to develop familiarity with paint in its many forms and confidence in its use. They should experience large- and small-scale work, different media and a variety of challenges. Keeping enjoyment and experimentation at the forefront of painting activities will help pupils gain mastery and dispel the frustration that some can experience at their own perceived lack of finesse.

Prior to Year 6, children will have had many occasions on which to refine their painting skills. They will have explored the potential of a host of media – including powder paints, tempera blocks, watercolours and liquid paints. In *Art Express* Book 5, children explored flower and plant forms through painting. They looked at examples of artists' work, identified common features and compared ideas about approaches to painting. They tried out different types of paint, made delicate watercolour paintings from observation of real flowers and followed this up with imaginative large-scale works, developing ideas of their own.

Still life provides the context for this unit, which enables pupils to further develop their skills in mixing and applying colour, creating different effects and making compositions. They will examine the conventions of still-life painting, consider artists' approaches and construct their own arrangements. They will increase their understanding of viewpoint, tone and complementary colour. They will use sketchbooks to make initial drawings from observation, share these in groups, select favourite compositions and finally make three paintings, using different media for each.

AIMS

This unit offers pupils the opportunity to:

- create imaginary and exploratory work, try out different approaches and develop an extended repertoire of ideas
- collect materials and ideas to develop in sketchbooks and explore different starting points
- consolidate and further develop skills in colour mixing, applying paint and selecting appropriate tools and materials for work on different scales and for different purposes
- use increased awareness of painting methods and styles to review and refine their own ideas, making connections with processes used by artists
- understand how particular materials and methods relate to context, and articulate their understanding and preferences with an increasingly specialist vocabulary.

ASSESSMENT FOR LEARNING

This unit provides many opportunities to assess progress – this should be ongoing and relate as much to pupils' understanding and behaviour as to what they produce. Observe the way in which pupils engage confidently (or not) with materials, their readiness to try new approaches and work in a team. Lastly, look for evidence that pupils have increased their grasp of the genre, and improved their ability to make informed choices and match different techniques to their purpose.

▶ CD-ROM RESOURCES

- Presentation: Introducing works of art to children – how, why and when
- Artworks and images
- Resource sheets:
    - Asking questions about still-life paintings
    - All about you…
    - Exploring texture in still life
    - Recommended still-life works
    - Colour wheel
- Teacher assessment
- Pupil self-evaluation

SESSION I **WHAT IS A STILL LIFE?**

LEARNING OBJECTIVES
Children will:

- learn to distinguish between different types of art by studying the conventions of still-life painting

- learn about art by becoming more aware of painting methods and styles, and how context influences materials and methods.

VOCABULARY **still life**, **traditional**, **modern**, **abstract**, **imaginary**, **natural**, **made**, **inanimate**, **composition**, **arrangement** and terms associated with the positioning and arrangement of objects within a still life

▼ RESOURCES

- ▶ a selection of still-life reproductions, postcards or images from books, calendars and so on
- ▶ individual whiteboards (or paper) and pens
- ▶ several downloaded images of still-life paintings, from the 17th to 20th centuries, to project onto an interactive whiteboard (see the National Gallery website – www.nationalgallery.org.uk/ collection/default_ online.htm – for many examples), as well as poster-sized reproductions for whole-class discussion
- ▶ one conventional still-life work to focus on in depth, for example, Luis Meléndez' *Still Life with Oranges and Walnuts* (see the CD-ROM)
- ▶ sketchbooks (one per child)
- ▶ CD-ROM: images of still-life paintings
- ▶ resource sheets: Recommended still-life works; Asking questions about still-life paintings

ACTIVITY

This session focuses on introducing pupils to the genre of still-life painting. It does not involve them in any actual painting but provides an opportunity to develop their understanding of a major genre, to initiate some higher order thinking and to provide a context for following sessions.

It includes an annotation activity that the children could do in class or as a homework task. Prior to the session, select some still-life works, ideally showing a wide range of subject matter and representing different time periods, from the 17th century onwards.

■ Start by handing out several postcards (or small pictures from books and calendars) per table. Allow pupils time to talk about and then list the content of the images on individual whiteboards or paper.

Ask the children to consider what the objects have in common and which ones appear frequently. See if they can group them and anticipate that they will notice the prevalence of food, flowers, natural objects, ordinary or household objects and so on. This activity works well when pupils pair up with a 'talking partner'. Ask pairs to come up with a definition of the term *still life*, and then get the pairs talking to one another more widely, to see whether they can agree.

■ Offer pupils a definition of still life, such as this one: 'a work of art depicting a collection or arrangement of inanimate objects', or this: 'usually set indoors, a grouping of inanimate objects that are positioned and then painted or drawn by an artist, often including fruit, bowls, flowers and books'. Explain the word *inanimate* if necessary, and then ask the children to think about what you would <u>not</u> find in a still-life painting. (You could

ask pupils to find more definitions as an independent activity later.)

■ Ask them to consider why artists might make still-life paintings and why certain objects might be chosen. Guide them to think about objects chosen for their shape, texture, pattern or colour, the choice of favourite possessions and the symbolic nature of certain objects. Encourage pupils to use descriptive as well as positional vocabulary to describe things in the picture.

■ Identify one image to focus on with the class and project this onto an interactive whiteboard. Using an example from the National Gallery website (see Resources) will enable the use of a zoom facility so individual aspects of the image can be drawn to the children's attention. Discuss it in detail, starting with questions relating to content; move on to composition and other qualities. Ask open-ended questions, *What do you think…?*, that will encourage reasoned answers and higher-order thinking from pupils.

Allow time for thought and encourage everyone to have a turn at speaking.

■ Choose a single image and stick it as a scan or a photocopy onto a double page of each child's sketchbook. Provide a series of questions (some examples are provided on the **Asking questions about still-life paintings** resource sheet) for them to respond to through notes, drawings, captions, annotations – in whatever form they like. Challenge the children to find interesting ways to express their responses. This task could be done as part of the session or for homework. The next session will start with a look at children's responses.

▼ ASSESSMENT FOR LEARNING

Can the children:
▶ talk specifically about features they observe in a selection of still-life paintings and, in more general terms, describe conventions of the genre using hypothesis?
▶ recognise common characteristics of paintings in relation to different contexts and talk about differences in methods and style using appropriate vocabulary?

DIFFERENTIATION

Children who have not progressed as far…
As this session is mostly about talking and sharing ideas, these pupils will benefit from being grouped with others who will allow them a voice in discussion. Alternatively, they could be paired sensitively with another child with whom to share their initial thoughts during the discussion activities.

Children who have progressed further…
These pupils may express their responses using more sophisticated vocabulary and make generalisations about the genre. Questioning will invite them to speculate and explain their answers and reasoning more fully. Challenge them to find out more by visiting one of the major art gallery websites (for example, that of the National Gallery).

SESSION 2 **CREATING A COMPOSITION**

LEARNING OBJECTIVES
Children will:

- learn to observe, record and generate new ideas by developing ideas from initial work in sketchbooks

- learn to evaluate and reflect by making connections between the processes they are engaged in and those explored by artists.

VOCABULARY composition, shape, position, viewpoint, overlapping, foreground, background, pattern, texture, shadow

▼ RESOURCES

- ▶ a varied selection of objects, enough for three or four still-life groups, for example, bottles, decorated plates, ornaments, patterned or plain fabrics, fruit, shells or other natural forms
- ▶ black water-based pens, different thicknesses
- ▶ viewfinders
- ▶ sketchbooks (one per child)
- ▶ tracing paper
- ▶ glue sticks
- ▶ small water pots
- ▶ fine brushes
- ▶ resource sheets: All about you…; Exploring texture in still life

ACTIVITY

In this session, pupils will think about how to arrange the different components within a still life, referring back to images they looked at in the previous session and then creating their own compositions. Stimulate discussion with questions such as: *What do you remember from our investigation of still life? What sort of objects did we see in still-life paintings? Why were these objects used?* The children will set up three or four small arrangements of objects and make drawings that comprise components of each.

■ Start by sharing ideas from the final task in Session 1. Highlight the different ways in which the children

have responded to the questions and the creative ways they found to present their thoughts on the page. Make it clear that you expected many of the questions you posed to generate different responses, and celebrate each child's individuality.

■ Show pupils several objects with differing characteristics, enough to make three or four arrangements. Talk about the importance of variety and elicit their thoughts about which ones should go together. Remind them of the sometimes strange combinations of objects they have looked at in reproductions of still-life paintings. Give the children time to talk in groups or with a partner and then let them take turns to make selections and assemble their chosen objects.

Encourage contrasting shapes, and varied heights, textures and colours, and invite them to articulate reasons for their choices. Encourage pupils to look at their arrangements from different viewpoints – straight on, from an oblique angle or from above. Talk about the choices artists make and suggest that they too will make those choices.

■ Ask each child to make a bold line drawing, with a black pen, of the objects in their nearest arrangement. Suggest that they focus on outline shapes and do not worry about detail. They can draw the whole arrangement or use a viewfinder to select a smaller area if they prefer.

■ When they have finished, move the children to a table closer to another arrangement and let them sketch in components of the new arrangement on the same page. Challenge them to choose objects with different shapes to complement those in their initial drawing. Some children could move on a second time when they have added more to their drawing.

■ Now ask pupils to swap sketchbooks with those from another table.

Give each child a sheet of tracing paper and ask them to trace a couple of shapes from someone else's sketchbook to add to their own. Once they have made a few tracings, they can return the books to their owners. Now show the children how to layer the traced drawings over their original sketchbook page, moving them around and finally sticking them down when they are satisfied with a particular arrangement.

■ Show pupils how to use a little water on a fine brush to add tone and depth to their drawings, looking especially at curved edges and shaded areas. Show them how to use the technique selectively and to make sure they use only a damp, not a dripping, brush.

■ The **All about you...** resource sheet provides an additional thinking and discussion activity for the children to do in pairs. The **Exploring texture in still life** resource sheet could equally be offered as a homework task.

DIFFERENTIATION

Children who have not progressed as far...
These pupils may make connections less readily between what they are doing and what artists before them have done and may find it harder to consider the different options open to them. They could be helped by working with a partner.

Children who have progressed further...
These pupils may demonstrate that they grasp the concept of artistic experimentation through the confident way in which they try alternative schemes for arranging their objects to create interesting compositions.

SESSION 3 **COLOUR AND TONE**

LEARNING OBJECTIVES
Children will:

- learn and consolidate their technical skills by creating tints and shades with paint through exploratory sketchbook work

- learn to develop, refine and apply their skills by experimenting purposefully with tonal values.

VOCABULARY **shade, tint, tone, lighter, darker, complementary**

▼ RESOURCES

- ▶ one or two still-life works with strongly contrasting tones
- ▶ sketchbooks (one per child)
- ▶ liquid ready-mixed or acrylic paint – one colour plus black and white, and a complementary colour
- ▶ water pots and palettes
- ▶ brushes – various sizes, flat-headed if possible
- ▶ still-life objects from Session 2
- ▶ strong anglepoise lamp or spotlight (optional)
- ▶ A2 or A3 sugar paper
- ▶ white chalk
- ▶ resource sheet: Colour wheel

ACTIVITY

In this session, the children will explore tinting and shading in their sketchbooks prior to making a simple tonal painting of their still-life arrangement. As there are two parts to the activity, they could be carried out in one extended session or over two sessions. You will need to set up an arrangement of still-life objects in the classroom for the second part.

- Explain to the class that *tone* describes the lightness or darkness of a colour and that this session will focus on exploring tone. They will almost certainly have explored tone before – it was introduced in the Painting unit of *Art Express* Book 2 – so they should be familiar with the process of adding colour incrementally. Demonstrate for the class the process of making a

tint by gradually adding small amounts of white paint to a strong colour, and the process of making a *shade* by adding small touches of black. Emphasise the difference that the tiniest smudge of black paint will make and advise caution. Let pupils experiment across a double page of their sketchbook, making whatever marks and patterns they choose and exploring the range of tones they can make with a single colour plus black and white.

- Direct the children's attention to the effects of light and shade on objects in the still-life arrangement – especially on curved surfaces. Point out dark, light and mid-tone areas of the composition and challenge pupils to think about the direction of the light source. If possible, shine a lamp or spotlight to one side of the arrangement so the children see strong shadows cast. Refer back to one or two artists' reproductions, especially any that show dramatic lighting and bold shadow effects.

- Now suggest pupils lightly sketch a few of the objects onto sugar paper with chalk and then begin to paint these using their single colour with black and white to emphasise light and shade. Stop the class partway through the session to review what they have done so far. Remind them to focus on creating the effects of light

and compare some of the different ways in which pupils are achieving this. Ask them to pause and consider their own piece of work or encourage them to ask a partner (a 'critical friend') to suggest any improvements they might make to it.

■ Discuss with the children how to use contrasting colours for the background and introduce the painterly notion of 'complementary colours' – red–green, blue–orange and yellow–violet. If pupils are not familiar with the colour wheel or need reminding, show them an example (see the **Colour wheel** resource sheet) and point out that the complementary colours sit opposite one another on the wheel. Explain that these colours are useful in a painting because, when placed side by side, they make one another appear more intense. Let the children try this for themselves and then paint in the background behind their still-life arrangement.

■ When all of their paintings are complete, allow pupils the opportunity to make comparisons between their own work and that of their classmates, to talk about what they have achieved over the course of the session, and what they most enjoyed as well as any difficulties they may have encountered.

▼ ASSESSMENT FOR LEARNING

Can the children:
▶ create a varied range of tones in exploratory sketchbook work?
▶ apply skills practised in sketchbooks in a painting to show light and shade within a composition?

DIFFERENTIATION

Children who have not progressed as far...
These pupils may find it challenging to apply light and dark tones to their compositions. Take a digital photograph of a still-life arrangement, download it and apply greyscale to show them the image purely in shades of black, white and grey – this can help them perceive and understand light and shade more clearly.

Children who have progressed further...
These pupils may grasp quite readily the processes of tinting and shading through incremental addition of black and white, and be able to apply it in relation to the source of light within their compositions.

SESSION 4 **THE EFFECTS OF COLOUR**

LEARNING OBJECTIVES
Children will:

■ develop imagination and creativity by experimenting with different materials, approaches and scale

■ develop a greater understanding of art by studying different painting methods and styles, and reflecting on their personal preferences.

VOCABULARY **primary, secondary, opaque, pastel, shade, tone, warm, cool, lighter, paler, complementary**

▼ RESOURCES

▸ sketchbook drawings made in Session 2
▸ still-life objects from Session 2
▸ cartridge or watercolour paper – A5 or smaller
▸ pencils
▸ fine-line pens
▸ watercolour paints or tempera blocks
▸ water pots and palettes
▸ small brushes
▸ CD-ROM: images of still-life paintings
▸ resource sheet: Recommended still-life works

ACTIVITY

In this session, pupils will explore the use of vibrant colour, pastel shades and colour families and see how different a composition can look when painted in different colour combinations.

■ Start by talking to the children about the difference that colour can make to an image. Remind them of some of the still-life paintings they have looked at from various periods in time and talk about ways in which colour affects mood and is used to different effects. Show a few examples: an early still life, for example, with dark, muted colours; another with a wide range of colours, shapes and textures; yet another in strong, bright colours or pastel shades. (Some examples are provided on the CD-ROM; otherwise, see suggestions on the **Recommended still-life works** resource sheet.) Explain to the class that they will make two or three small still-life compositions based on their drawings from Session 2 and then paint them using different colour combinations so that they can compare these to one another.

■ Redistribute the drawings and some small rectangles of heavy paper or card. Show pupils how they can create a new design, taking elements from their previous drawings and then rearranging them however they please. Allow time for them to draft at least two versions of their new composition – and then they can start to paint. Encourage the children to talk to one other about the colour choices they are planning or suggest they work in pairs and share a palette, which will require them to share their decision-making. As these are small-scale paintings, pupils will be better using watercolour tins or tempera or poster paints with small brushes.

■ Stop the class from time to time in the course of the painting to reflect on what they have done so far and to hold up examples that other pupils may use to extend their own repertoire. Draw particular attention to the effect of different colourways and encourage the children to use vocabulary as suggested above. Remind them that they could explore shades of a single colour, pale pastel tones, clashing complementary colours, cool wintry or warm autumnal colours and so on. They can also vary the way they apply the paint – laying it on in delicate washes, in bold, flat patches or in a mixture of intensities. The children may have time, depending on the length of the session, to make two or three of these small paintings and thus to explore several options.

■ At the end of the session, spread out the paintings on a table and encourage the children, with a talking partner or in small groups, to talk about their experiences. Ask them to identify those that they think are most successful, giving reasons for their choices, and to express their overall preference. If time permits, ask pupils to talk about how they might change their work in a subsequent session.

▼ ASSESSMENT FOR LEARNING

Can the children:
▶ create a composition and confidently experiment with different combinations of colours, arriving at a conclusion they are pleased with?
▶ describe and evaluate differences in methods and style using appropriate vocabulary and expressing reasoned preferences?

DIFFERENTIATION

Children who have not progressed as far...
These pupils may be less forthcoming about expressing preferences in a whole-class situation but may be supported by working with a partner, sharing a palette and making joint decisions about the range of colours to explore.

Children who have progressed further...
These pupils may experiment with a more varied range of approaches in their work and talk confidently about the differences they observe. They should be encouraged to make analogies with what they have seen in artists' still-life paintings.

SESSION 5 **FROM ANOTHER VIEWPOINT**

LEARNING OBJECTIVES

Children will:

- extend their imagination and creativity by experimenting with different approaches and expanding their repertoire of ideas

- learn more about art by making connections between the materials and processes used by artists and those explored by themselves.

VOCABULARY See Sessions 2 and 4

▼ RESOURCES

- ▸ still-life objects provided and arranged by the children
- ▸ reproductions (or digital images) of work by a chosen still-life painter – for example, Patrick Caulfield
- ▸ heavy cartridge paper or card – large sheets
- ▸ pencils
- ▸ tempera block, ready-mixed or acrylic paints in the following colours: two blues (cobalt or Prussian blue, ultramarine or brilliant blue), two reds (vermillion and crimson), two yellows (brilliant yellow and lemon yellow), and white
- ▸ palettes, mixing plates, water containers
- ▸ a range of brushes
- ▸ permanent marker pens
- ▸ CD-ROM: images of still-life paintings
- ▸ pupil self-evaluation sheet

ACTIVITY

In this last session, pupils will make large paintings incorporating their own objects and artefacts brought from home, and loosely inspired by looking at still-life images. The children will need to be primed beforehand to bring in a small item from home to contribute to the still life – for example, a small ornament, pot, plate or vase, or a piece of patterned fabric. In this example, pupils are introduced to a collection of paintings and prints made by the English artist Patrick Caulfield but also, as a means of comparison, to works by European artists such as Fernand Léger, Juan Gris and Giorgio Morandi.

■ Start by showing the class, and letting them talk about, some examples of 20th-century still-life paintings (see the CD-ROM). Focus on how objects are positioned – in simple linear arrangements (Morandi), randomly overlapped (the Cubist works of Léger and Gris) or seen from a range of different viewpoints (Caulfield). Draw attention also to the use of colour and texture, from Morandi's muted and subtle colour shifts to the bold outlines and strong, unmodulated colour of Caulfield.

■ Now spend a little longer looking at Caulfield's paintings and prints, many of which show very ordinary subjects (jugs, wine glasses, table lamps) and

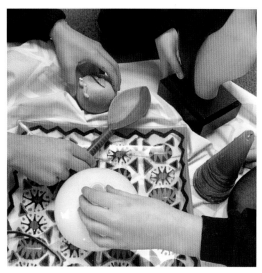

have the appearance of painted signs or commercial advertising hoardings, because of the way in which the artist eliminated all but the barest of detail. Point out the absence of brush marks and the limited palette of bright bold colours surrounded by black outlines. Look especially at Caulfield's 1969 painting *Pottery*, which shows jugs, plates and vases depicted from different viewpoints – some painted as though seen from above, some near the

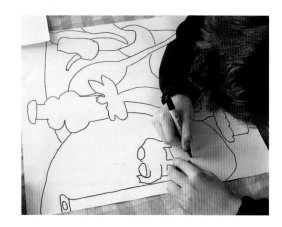

centre viewed from eye level and others near the top shown from beneath. Caulfield himself described this painting as 'an excuse for me to use a lot of colour'.

■ Now ask groups of children to make small arrangements from the objects they brought in. They can do this on a board or table top or in a small cardboard box with the top and one side removed, like a stage set. Make sure there are extra objects available and fabric on which to place them. Ask pupils to draft their own composition from these arrangements, looking at a range of viewpoints, as in Caulfield's painting. Encourage the children to superimpose the objects in any way they like to fill the space, and not to worry about getting the scale right. They can use Caulfield's style of outlining shapes with paint or with marker pens. Give pupils a free choice of colours to use, and stop them now and then during the process to stand back from their work and look at the balance of those they have chosen.

■ When the paintings are complete, bring the children together to look at the whole class set. Pose questions that make them think about their own work but also develop awareness of how others have produced different responses to the same activity.

Recap on the processes the children have engaged in, in both this and the previous sessions, and ask them to reflect on their progress and outcomes with a talking partner. They can also talk through the **Pupil self-evaluation** sheet to review their progress over the course of this unit.

DIFFERENTIATION

Children who have not progressed as far…
Either these pupils may draft simple compositions using a less extensive range of shapes, or an adult could help them to move traced drawings around in different ways to make objects overlap and fill the page.

Children who have progressed further…
In this final piece of work, these pupils may synthesise more readily their personal ideas with their developing knowledge and understanding of the conventions of modern still-life painting. They could research more about late 20th-century still life from the internet, in school or for homework.

OTHER AREAS OF LEARNING

GEOGRAPHY

- Look in detail at a painting such as 'Luis Meléndez' *Still Life with Oranges and Walnuts*' and focus specifically on containers and packaging. Consider the materials that were available in the 18th century and today's alternatives.
- Look at paintings by Juan Sánchez Cotán, Luis Meléndez or Willem Kalf. Consider the geographical provenance of foods depicted and the influence of climate. Collect some similar objects and take digital photos of them to compare.

ART AND DESIGN

- Children could paint their own collage papers in strong, opaque colours and, once dry, cut out simple shapes to arrange as a still life.
- Construct simple objects for a still life arrangement from box card or corrugated card. Children can cut, score, join, slot together and arrange their shapes - then draw or photograph their compositions.

SCIENCE

- Children discussing a traditional still-life painting of fruit and vegetables can make links to work on healthy diet within 'Life processes and living things'. They can compare produce seen in the paintings with comparable produce today and create modern, 'healthy' still life arrangements to photograph.

PHYSICAL, SOCIAL AND HEALTH EDUCATION (PSHE)

- Encourage social skills, listening and collaboration by playing a form of the I-Spy game, with children in a group taking turns to identify something in a still-life reproduction. They should start with very literal observations and be encouraged to look for finer detail, expanding their ideas to make more extended contributions.
- Explore emotions through engaging with works of art that portray particular moods.
- Encourage collaborative working, sharing and problem-solving and prompt pupils to act as 'critical friends' to one another.

Painting

MATHEMATICS

- Can pupils employ mathematical language, especially positional vocabulary, to describe the whereabouts of objects within a still life and to describe flat and solid shapes, in addition to using descriptive and artistic terms?

LITERACY

- Look at a collection of a dozen or more still-life images (postcards, reproductions or on an interactive whiteboard) and invite pupils to debate, in a group, which six should be chosen for an exhibition. Ask them to justify choices and use persuasive argument.
- Ask pairs of children to write a short catalogue entry about a particular still life to attract buyers at an art auction. To encourage a sale, their description and the language they use must be very persuasive.

ICT

- Set children some internet research from a gallery website such as the National Gallery or allow them to choose their own area of interest. They could, for example, research 16th–18th century paintings on food to discover what people ate and what such paintings show about wealth and poverty.
- Children could import a few still-life objects into an art programme and then manipulate them into different arrangements.

The magic of printmaking is that it is exciting, immediate and cheap! The invention of the printing press could arguably be one of the most important human inventions. It allowed images and text to be reproduced and made available to a mass audience. However, making prints by hand without a press is also a valuable means of creating marks and patterns. Today, we take for granted the ways in which we can transmit images by email or the web, or the immediacy of making copies on printers and copiers. Traditional hand-carved, wooden printing blocks, however, are still used around the world to print images onto fabric or paper. This unit combines both ancient and modern to create a unique design.

Prior to Year 5, pupils will have explored materials and media to make simple prints ranging from basic finger or handprints to monotype or printing blocks. They will also have begun to make connections between their work and that of artists/printmakers from around the world. You are advised to use the sessions in *Art Express* Book 5 as an introduction to printmaking before attempting this unit.

Exploring ornamentation and pattern allows a connection with the way in which, throughout history, pattern has been used to decorate, enhance and enrich objects. Pattern can be seen embroidered on fabric, painted on tiles, printed on wallpaper, woven in carpets, inlaid in wood, carved in stone, etched into glass and engraved in metal.

This unit focuses on pattern and design. Pupils will create a design that will be repeated, rotated and have aspects of symmetry. They will make a block and print onto a range of surfaces, including fabric, papers and books, to create decorative objects, alongside using a photocopier – as well as using a computer, if desired – to create a series of contemporary prints.

AIMS

This unit offers pupils the opportunity to:

■ use a sketchbook to collect and select materials, to try out alternative ideas and designs before reaching a decision, and to develop drawings into ideas for printed images

■ design a pattern for a printing block, and plan and explore several alternatives before arriving at a final design, if possible using computers and digital cameras to record ideas

■ compare and contrast examples of pattern from different contexts and develop an increased understanding of repetition, rotation and symmetry in printed designs

■ recognise how printed pattern has been used historically and culturally in different ways and for different purposes.

ASSESSMENT FOR LEARNING

In this unit, assessment should be ongoing. Keep all the initial sketches, ideas, designs, photographs and ICT work, as well as the final pattern printed by hand and machine. By collating all these investigations, you will gain a good indication of the journey undertaken. Do pupils show an understanding of the mathematical aspects of pattern design? Can they select a final design and justify their decision? Do they show an increased awareness of pattern in their own environment? Use these questions alongside your classroom observations and the pupil self-evaluation sheet.

▶ CD-ROM RESOURCES

- Presentation: Making relief printing blocks Masterclass
- Artworks and images
- Resource sheets:
  - Victorian design
  - Pattern, motif and shapes
  - Tile design
  - Complementary colours
  - Using ICT to make and print tile designs
- Teacher assessment
- Pupil self-evaluation

SESSION I **EXPLORING PATTERN – THE VICTORIAN DESIGNERS**

LEARNING OBJECTIVES

Children will:

- understand how different elements (shapes, designs, motifs) are repeated and combined to create a pattern
- learn to observe and record patterns in their environment using a sketchbook
- learn how printed pattern has been used historically and culturally in different ways and for different purposes, with a focus on Victorian Britain.

VOCABULARY aesthetic, **pattern**, **motif**, **Victorian**, **Medieval**, **rotation**, **reflection**, **symmetrical**, **repetition**, **border**

▼ RESOURCES

- ▸ sketchbooks
- ▸ viewfinders
- ▸ Indian woodcut printing blocks or old wooden lettering (alternatively, make some potato printing blocks or use pieces of wood, sticks and other objects as stamps)
- ▸ inking trays, printing rollers and water-based ink
- ▸ CD-ROM: images of man-made patterns; images of patterns in nature; examples of printed textiles, papers and tiles; images of Arts and Crafts design
- ▸ resource sheet: Victorian design

ACTIVITY

Prior to the session, ask pupils to bring in real examples of patterns from home (for example, fabrics, wallpaper, tiles) and from nature (such as honeycomb, shells, butterfly wings, seeds, fruit). Some images are also provided on the CD-ROM.

- Discuss the word *pattern*. Make a list on the board of types of pattern, referring to the images and objects collected by the class. Examples might include: geometric, abstract, natural form, lettering; pattern that is raised or on the surface, carved into wood, printed on paper, inlaid, engraved, woven into textiles, painted on; designed in architecture; stone circles, ancient settlements and aerial photographs of fields.
- Compare the man-made patterns with patterns found in nature. Use sketchbooks to record the differences and similarities, through annotation and drawings. Viewfinders could be used to focus on specific parts of a pattern. Discuss the findings as a class.
- Talk about the words *shape* and *motif* (in a repeated design). Investigate patterns that use abstract shapes and others that may be based on plants, animals or other objects.
- Show the children a range of printing blocks, ideally Indian woodcut blocks or old wooden lettering. Alternatively, in advance, make some potato blocks, or use pieces of wood,

straws or shapes that you can dip into ink or paint. Encourage pupils to experiment with printing them onto paper to explore pattern. Ask, *Can you use more than one design to create a pattern? How do you make the pattern repeat? Can it repeat in different directions?* This activity will reinforce previous work on pattern, and hopefully ask new questions about how patterns can be created.

- Bring the class back together and examine the images of printed textiles and papers on the CD-ROM. Compare the shapes, motifs and patterns from different periods and cultures. In some cultures, pattern is used to display

status or cultural identity. The colours and patterns of Scottish tartans, for example, are clan-specific. Patterns can be tattooed or painted directly onto the skin as a rite of passage or as a manifestation of the wearer's status within a cultural group. Pattern can be symbolic to the wearer, tell a story or have pure aesthetic purpose. The latter was the case for the artists and craftspeople of the Arts and Crafts Movement in Victorian Britain.
Ask, *What does 'aesthetic' mean? When were the Victorian times?*

■ Discuss the Arts and Crafts Movement and the artists and craftspeople working in this period (such as William Morris, Burne-Jones, Pugin, De Morgan). Look at the use of pattern in their designs (see the CD-ROM). What aspects of nature did

they include in their work? Look at how the different elements (shapes, designs, motifs) are repeated and combined to create a pattern. How did they use pattern?

■ Use the **Victorian design** resource sheet to research the Arts and Crafts Movement. In sketchbooks, record a range of Victorian design patterns from fabrics, books, postcards and real tiles, if possible. Try to make links with local sites (for example, churches or houses) that have examples of Victorian tiles or decoration, using the internet, books, photographs or a local visit (this could be set as a homework activity). The results of this research will be used in Session 2.

■ In preparation for Session 2, begin to discuss the ways in which patterns are made, such as through the use of repetition, overlapping, rotation, reflection and translation.

▼ ASSESSMENT FOR LEARNING

Can the children:
▸ describe different ways in which patterns can be made and recognise that a pattern is created when a design, motif or shape is repeated?
▸ recognise natural and man-made patterns in their environment and record them through sketches and annotations in a sketchbook?
▸ talk about how the Arts and Crafts Movement used pattern?

DIFFERENTIATION

Children who have not progressed as far...
Split the class into groups, to feed back ideas into the discussion. Ensure that each child has the opportunity to contribute something, written, verbal or drawn. Provide support with explanations of techniques and vocabulary.

Children who have progressed further...
Encourage higher-order thinking by asking these pupils to research pattern further, using more sophisticated, accurate vocabulary. Ask them to consider the following:
Why is pattern important in art and design? What makes a pattern? Can they find examples of pattern in artists' work they have studied? What materials can be used to create pattern?

SESSION 2 **DESIGNING A MOTIF FOR A PATTERN**

LEARNING OBJECTIVES

Children will:

- learn how to use their imagination to explore possibilities and generate ideas by developing their drawings into ideas for printed images

- develop their capacity to plan and explore alternatives before arriving at a final design
- learn more about the patterns of the Arts and Crafts Movement and increase understanding of repetition, rotation and symmetry.

VOCABULARY tonal, observational, symmetry, repetition, rotation, translation, motif, asymmetrical, bold

▼ RESOURCES

- ▸ natural objects, such as flowers, fruit and seeds
- ▸ sketchbooks
- ▸ 2B or 4B pencils
- ▸ viewfinders
- ▸ tracing paper
- ▸ thin black felt-tip pens
- ▸ CD-ROM:
    sample tile;
    images of Arts and
    Crafts designs;
    images of tiles
- ▸ resource sheets:
    Pattern, motif and shapes;
    Tile design

ACTIVITY

In this session, pupils will look at how patterns are created and use this information to make their own motif for a tile design. Prior to the session, gain a better understanding of how patterns are formed by creating your own tile design, or print out and photocopy the sample tile from the CD-ROM.

- Start by sharing the Victorian design research from Session 1. Show examples of William Morris's wallpaper and fabric designs (see the CD-ROM). Recap on the use of nature in Arts and Crafts designs. Ask, *Why are some designs more striking than others? How can you make a design asymmetrical?*

- Collect a range of flowers, fruit and seeds. Ask the children to create a series of observational drawings in sketchbooks, based on these natural objects, in preparation for their tile design. Focus on the decorative nature of the objects and use 2B or 4B pencils to create areas of tone. Discuss how they are making these drawings: *Are you drawing the whole thing or selecting parts? Are you interested in the fine detail or the shapes? What patterns can you see in your objects?*

- Remind pupils of the discussion in Session 1 on the definition of patterns and their repetitive nature. Distribute the **Pattern, motif and shapes** resource sheet and ask the children to identify which patterns show symmetry, repetition, rotation,

translation and motif. Are the designs abstract or based on nature? Can they date the design? Show the images of tiles from the CD-ROM and look for examples of symmetry, repetition and rotation. Show the children patterns based on square designs, repeated and reflected, or rotated. Can they identify the single design element that has been used to create the pattern?

■ Review the observational drawings with the class (lay them out on a table). Show pupils how to use a viewfinder to select interesting sections or motifs for their tile design, and then use small pieces of tracing paper to select different parts of the drawings. Ask them to transfer these shapes onto the **Tile design** resource sheet to create two different 10cm x 10cm designs.

■ Demonstrate to pupils how a design that is not centred produces a more dynamic pattern when repeated and rotated. Discuss the various shapes and patterns used within the design and how their positioning affects the overall pattern.

■ Once a design has been drawn, ask the children to outline it using a thin black felt-tip pen. Encourage the use of bold shapes to create strong positive and negative areas. Remind them that bold designs with large dark and light areas will create exciting and dynamic patterns.

■ Pair pupils up as 'talking partners' to discuss the tile designs. *Which one do they like? Have they created designs using large, bold elements? Is their design asymmetrical? Which would work well as a final design?* Each child then needs to select one tile for development and use appropriate vocabulary and considered reasons to justify their choice in their sketchbook.

■ The final design needs to be carefully traced onto a piece of tracing paper, ready to make a printing block in Session 3. This will be printed in one colour; some pupils may feel they need to simplify their design. Their black and white design will need to be photocopied for Session 4, so make sure that it is named!

▼ ASSESSMENT FOR LEARNING

Can the children:
▶ use their own observational drawings to create a design?
▶ produce two completely different designs and select one for development and justify their choice?
▶ create designs using rotation and symmetry effectively and make links to designs they have studied?

DIFFERENTIATION

Children who have not progressed as far...
Help these pupils select interesting shapes for a design using viewfinders and tracing paper. Photocopy their initial design so they can see how it will repeat or use ICT to show how this will work. Where possible, do practical demonstrations for these children.

Children who have progressed further...
These pupils can use a wider range of tone within their observational drawings. Encourage them to use line expressively and to visualise how their design will repeat if rotated or reflected. Can they describe the amount of turn through which a shape has rotated and the direction? They could use ICT to create more sophisticated designs.

SESSION 3 **PRINTING DESIGNS BY HAND**

LEARNING OBJECTIVES

Children will:

- learn to design patterns of increasing complexity by studying how repetition, rotation and symmetry are used in printed designs
- develop further technical skills
- learn to reflect, adapt and refine their ideas by engaging with others.

VOCABULARY **printing block**, **inking up**, **rotation**, **symmetry**

▼ RESOURCES

- ▶ neoprene sheets, cut to 10cm x 10cm, self-adhesive if possible (sometimes called 'Funky Foam') – or card or sugar paper (refer to the Masterclass, or to the Printing unit in *Art Express* Book 5)
- ▶ tracing paper
- ▶ 2B pencils
- ▶ thin black marker pens (optional)
- ▶ scissors
- ▶ thick card (mill-board is ideal) as a base, cut to the size of block, 10cm x 10cm, or adjust to fit
- ▶ PVA Medium glue and spreaders (if neoprene is not self-adhesive)
- ▶ rollers
- ▶ water-based printing ink (can be used on fabric, but do not wash – use fabric printing ink if washing is required)
- ▶ inking trays or surface to roll the ink out onto
- ▶ newspaper or newsprint to cover tables
- ▶ A2 (or larger) paper
- ▶ card, paper or fabric to print onto (sheeting or calico)
- ▶ Presentation: Making relief printing blocks Masterclass (see section on Neoprene foam print method)
- ▶ CD-ROM: images of Arts and Crafts design; images of tiles

ACTIVITY

Prior to this session, use the **Making relief printing blocks** Masterclass to recap on how to make, ink up and print a block. You may need to break this session up into making the block first, and printing later, as, depending on the experience of the class, you may need more time to experiment.

- Remind pupils of the printing experience from Session 1. Discuss printmaking, and talk about the different ways in which a design can be transferred to fabric or paper. Show examples of hand-made prints on fabric or paper (see the CD-ROM) and talk about how this is more time-consuming and perhaps more difficult than modern printing techniques.
- Talk about the different surfaces the children could decorate with their prints, such as sheets of wallpaper, fabric, cards, books or even tiles.
- The card and neoprene relief block will be similar to a woodcut or lino – the raised areas (neoprene) will take colour and the blank (card) areas beneath will remain white. It may be worth showing this to pupils with scrap pieces of neoprene. (If they made fish collograph blocks in the Printing unit of *Art Express* Book 5, they should be familiar with this process.)
- Demonstrate how to use the tracing paper copy (made in Session 2) to transfer the design to the neoprene, by turning it over and drawing carefully along the outline. If the pencil outline is hard to see, go over it using a permanent marker pen.
- Cut out the different shapes, arrange them on the cardboard base and stick them down. If the neoprene is not self-adhesive, use PVA Medium glue (it must dry before printing).
- This design will be one colour for simplicity. Select a colour and show how to ink up the printing block and press down the design onto the paper

(use a clean roller to add more pressure if required).

■ Initially, pupils should work on large sheets of paper until a final design is found. Ask them to place an arrow on the back of the card (it does not matter at this stage which way up it is). Then ask them to make a series of four prints, with the arrow pointing in different directions – 12, 3, 6, and 9 o'clock – and label these as such. This will give an indication of the effects of rotation to their design. Next, print four tiles in a square with the arrow facing the same way.

Encourage other experimentation with the printing block.
■ Finally, print a whole sheet of the design onto paper, changing the orientation as part of the design (see the illustration, right). Then print onto fabric, tissue or objects, as decided as a class. The children could combine tiles to create different patterns and designs, or use all the tiles to create a border around other pieces of work. It may work well to pair pupils up so they can help each other if they are printing a large area of paper or fabric.
■ Review the printing at the end of the session and discuss the types of pattern that have been created. Some pupils may want to create further designs after the next session and reprint their block – just allow the ink to dry or wipe it carefully away with a baby wipe. Do not wash!

▼ ASSESSMENT FOR LEARNING

Can the children:
▸ create a printing block using their initial design and successfully print this onto a range of materials?
▸ make links to the patterns studied previously and show understanding of rotation, repetition and symmetry in their work?
▸ discuss with a partner their findings and make suggestions about how to improve work?

DIFFERENTIATION

Children who have not progressed as far...
This activity is much easier if self-adhesive neoprene is used. These pupils may find working in reverse difficult – trace another copy of the design onto the cardboard base using the tracing paper, so that the pieces can be laid in place.

Children who have progressed further...
These pupils could make a multi-coloured pattern, printing with a block for each colour, one on top of the another, and with the lightest colour first. Alternatively, the original tile could be reduced to 5cm x 5cm on the photocopier and children can use tracing paper to create a new design, rotating and reflecting this tile to make a new 10cm x 10cm image.

SESSION 4 **PRINTING USING A PHOTOCOPIER**

LEARNING OBJECTIVES
Children will:

- develop imagination and creativity by using colour to express ideas about harmony and contrast within a design
- learn that designing requires a disciplined approach by planning and exploring several alternatives before arriving at a final design
- gain confidence in analysing art by observing how the application of colour to selected areas highlights those areas and emphasises their importance within the design.

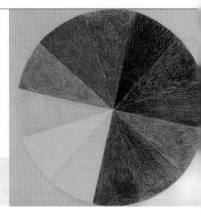

VOCABULARY **complementary colours**, **contrasting**, **harmony**, **highlight**, **emphasis**

▼ RESOURCES

- ▸ 18 copies (16 plus 2 samples) per child of their final design from Session 2
- ▸ coloured pencils in a range of complementary and contrasting colours – good quality, if available (blendable pencils are excellent but expensive)
- ▸ large envelopes – one per child (use old ones and rename)
- ▸ CD-ROM: images of Arts and Crafts design
- ▸ resource sheet: Complementary colours; Using ICT to make and print tile designs

ACTIVITY

In advance of the session, photocopy the tile designs from Session 2 (see Resources). (This may seem like a huge amount of photocopying, but you can fit six designs onto an A3 sheet, which works out to three A3 sheets per child.) When you cut out the tiles to distribute to the class, leave a little white paper around each one – this makes it easier to apply colour neatly. Store the photocopied tiles in named envelopes until required.

■ Hand out the photocopies and ask the children to compare them (modern printing) with the hand-made prints from Session 3. Ask, *What are the differences? Which do you prefer? What are the benefits of one over the other?* Talk about modern printing of books and papers and compare with the medieval Gutenberg press.

■ The children are going to add colour by hand – much like the artists who added colour to engravings of famous works of art in the 19th century, making it possible for 'ordinary' people

to have artwork in their homes.

■ Revisit the CD-ROM images of Arts and Crafts design, discussing the colour schemes and how a motif could be created in a series of different colours – like wallpaper designs today.

■ Show pupils a colour wheel (see the **Complementary colours** resource sheet). Discuss how colours facing each other on the colour wheel complement each other by making both colours appear brighter and more vivid, while colours that lie next to

! TEACHING TIP
If you are short of time, you can turn the tiles into monochrome versions before photocopying – colour the areas of contrast with a black felt-tip pen, photocopy as above but skip this session and move on to Session 5.

each other appear less strong, but have a harmonious effect. If this is a new concept to your class, spend time exploring this in sketchbooks with coloured pencils or coloured papers.

■ It may be worth recapping how to get the most effective colour from coloured pencils. Use sketchbooks to explore and ask, *How do you get a more intense colour? Do you colour in one direction, with a ruler or scribble?* Investigate the most effective means.

■ Now encourage the children to experiment with colours on the two spare tiles. They can shade them in, using colours to make contrasts, harmonies or a combination of the two. These tiles can then be stuck into sketchbooks as reference. Suggest that pupils use limited colours on one and more free ideas on the other. *What do they notice? Which do they prefer?* Ask

them to record their findings in their sketchbook along the way.

■ Ask the children to focus on selecting their final colour scheme. Remind them that they will need to add colour to all 16 tiles and that the nature of pattern is that the same design needs to be repeated, so they must apply the same colours to the same areas on each tile. They will need to select one colour and apply it to their chosen area on all the tiles before selecting the next colour to apply to a different area on all the tiles. This will cut down on the number of coloured pencils required and keep the activity more focused.

■ The coloured tiles will need to be trimmed for the next session with a rotary trimmer. Keep the tiles in a book or under a weight to stop the edges from curling up.

▼ ASSESSMENT FOR LEARNING

Can the children:
▶ identify primary and secondary colours that interact with each other to create harmonies and contrasts?
▶ make informed choices when selecting and applying colours to their design?
▶ explain how a design might change if different colours were used?

! VARIATIONS

Colouring could be done for homework or at different times during the school week. You could skip the colouring-in process and opt to use ICT to create the tiles. Either scan the original coloured tile or use the black and white photocopy scanned in or photographed, and then add colour using a paint package. Print out 16 further tiles. These options use a lot of ink but will give professional results! In another variation, children could use different methods of colouring – felt-tip pens, watercolour paints and so on.

DIFFERENTIATION

Children who have not progressed as far...
These pupils could work together on a combined design to produce a group piece. Different members of the group would be responsible for adding different colours to the work. You could restrict the number of tiles to four or eight, but having more gives a greater understanding of the properties of pattern.

Children who have progressed further...
These pupils could use ICT to create a design, add colour or vary rotation and symmetry. They could experiment with more complex designs and solutions, applying the **Using ICT to make and print tile designs** resource sheet to explore options with *Microsoft Publisher*. Invite them to relate their work with rotation to mathematics by describing the direction and amount of turn in degrees.

SESSION 5 **SELECTING A FINAL DESIGN**

LEARNING OBJECTIVES
Children will:

- develop and refine technical skills and understanding
- reinforce their understanding of the value of planning systematically by making good use of time and resources

- further develop the capacity to review and evaluate aspects of their own and others' work
- develop and extend their understanding and appreciation of the complexity of repetition, rotation and symmetry.

VOCABULARY **rotation, reflection, symmetrical, asymmetrical, repetition, shape, space, motif, translation**

▼ RESOURCES

- ▸ sketchbooks
- ▸ coloured and trimmed designs from Session 4
- ▸ glue stick or pot of PVA Medium for each pair
- ▸ large sheets of black sugar paper
- ▸ digital cameras (if available)
- ▸ CD-ROM: examples of printed textiles, papers and tiles; images of Arts and Crafts design
- ▸ resource sheets: Pattern, motifs and shapes; Using ICT to make and print tile designs
- ▸ pupil self-evaluation sheet

ACTIVITY

Look back at the patterns from the CD-ROM and those collected in Session 1, as well as the printed designs that were created in Session 3. Discuss the different combinations and how the design is often a motif that is repeated in different ways. Identify patterns using repetition, rotation and reflection, and look at alternative patterns created using the same design. Use the **Pattern, motifs and shapes** resource sheet to revisit these combinations.

■ Using black sugar paper as a background on the table, ask pupils to use their tiles in a variety of ways to create a selection of patterns using repetition, rotation and/or reflection. Stop after the first arrangement and pair the children up to work with a partner. Can they recognise especially effective elements in each others' work and suggest possible alterations or improvements using some of the pattern- and colour-related vocabulary they have encountered over the course of this unit?

■ Use digital cameras throughout to record the arrangements (use a label with name and number, for example, James H 1, so images can be correlated later). Pupils can continue to work either on their own or with a partner to record the different patterns, until they are happy with their final design. Encourage the use of sketchbooks throughout to make notes, and record observations and combinations. Challenge the class to think about and discuss the following: *Why are 16 tiles being used? Could you have used eight? What might have happened? Could you use an odd number? What happens if you use four? And so on…*

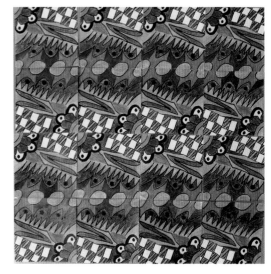

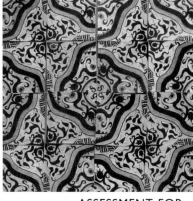

■ Ask pupils to stick their final pattern design onto black sugar paper. Ensure they take care when assembling their patterns – each square must be placed perfectly to prevent gaps, which would interrupt the design. Working in pairs is effective because one child can apply glue while the other sticks.

■ Display all patterns and encourage the children to talk about each other's work, highlighting areas they feel are effective, comparing approaches and talking about their own work and how it might be adapted or improved.

■ Each child will produce a pattern design 40cm x 40cm (or an equivalent area, if you choose a different initial shape or size.) Lay out the final designs and ask the children to complete the **Pupil self-evaluation** sheet with a partner.

■ This activity will create an eye-catching display, particularly effective when viewed from a distance, such as in a school hall or down a corridor.

■ In a future session, revisit the excellent patterns that were created in the last session and look at the photographs taken of all the different combinations on the whiteboard. If possible, stick examples of these combinations into sketchbooks to record the process. Discuss with the class the decisions they made and why they liked their final pattern best.

■ Look at the **Using ICT to make and print tile designs** resource sheet to explore pattern-making using *Microsoft Word* or *Publisher*.

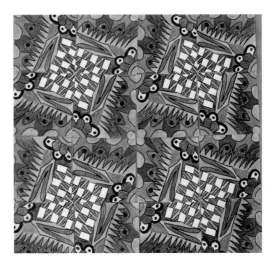

▼ ASSESSMENT FOR LEARNING

Can the children:
▶ design a range of patterns using their motif and record these in a variety of ways?
▶ constructively comment on their own and others' work?
▶ consider their own and classmates' final patterns and comment constructively on the initial tile design, use of colour and placement of tiles, and how they have affected the overall pattern?
▶ use appropriate vocabulary to describe different uses of repetition, rotation and symmetry in their own and others' work?

DIFFERENTIATION

Children who have not progressed as far...
These pupils may find this level of precision challenging when arranging and sticking down their tiles. They could work with an adult or with a more able pupil. Use digital cameras to record different combinations and break this activity down into smaller sessions.

Children who have progressed further...
Suggest that these pupils try up to eight different arrangements before they select their final design. They should be encouraged to use the appropriate vocabulary to explain their combinations. Some pupils may be able to explore different colourways and tessellation using computers and simple art software.

OTHER AREAS OF LEARNING

LITERACY

- Ask pupils to write stories and poems in a range of different patterns, for example, a poem about a whirlwind set in a spiral shape.
- Invite the children to use repeating sounds and words to create a 'rhythmic poem', or to incorporate repeated letters into a piece of artwork.

HISTORY

- Ask pupils to investigate the use of pattern through history, comparing different periods and finding out how people used pattern in everyday life and to decorate significant things.
- Look at how architects and designers have used initials, emblems and motifs, for example, on crowns, buildings and furnishings.

ART AND DESIGN

- Look at the use of pattern in advertising and as an important design tool.
- Research templates and patterns in engineering and machinery.
- Investigate how tiles are made. What materials are used? How is the image printed onto or pressed into the tile?

Printing

MATHEMATICS

- Challenge pupils to visualise and predict the position of a shape following a rotation, reflection or translation.
- Ask the children to look at architecture from around the world and see if they can find examples of tessellation and geometric design. Links could be made to other areas of study including the Romans and Islamic art.

SCIENCE

- Challenge pupils to find patterns in nature, for example, in webs, plants, rocks, sediments, rivers and erosion.
- Children can find out about fractal patterns that occur naturally throughout nature (look at shells, pine cones or the petals of some flowers, for example). Show them also Paisley patterns and fabric designs from India that use fractals.

ICT

- Use ICT to design and repeat patterns.
- Pupils can scan in their pattern designs and add colour, rotate, flip or add layers.

It is impossible to conceive of a life without cloth. It touches us almost constantly. Our homes are full of it, it is used for practical and aesthetic purposes, and we see, feel and use it every day. Similarly, it forms a part of almost every culture in the world. It is bound up in our history, and offers valuable and fascinating links with all curriculum areas.

Prior to Year 6, pupils will have built on their knowledge of cloth, its use and properties, as well as their understanding of its significance in society and its importance to us. They will have developed an awareness of the role of cloth in different countries and cultures. It is expected that they will have experienced weaving on a rectangular card loom, experimented with ways of manipulating fabric, and used a needle and thread, but if this is not the case, previous units of *Art Express* can be used to introduce or revisit these skills. In *Art Express* Book 5, children learned to experiment creatively with fabric, threads and wools, and used stitching to produce different visual effects.

During the course of this unit, a wealth of opportunities are offered for Year 6 pupils to build on this knowledge and understanding, but working at a more sophisticated level to explore further the properties and possibilities of this very versatile medium. The children will explore the traditional processes of weaving and felting to create their own fabrics, and discover additional ways of colouring, patterning and embellishing cloth through manipulation, batik, painting, stitching and beading. The CD-ROM provides a variety of images to inspire experimentation and support the learning in each session.

AIMS

This unit offers pupils the opportunity to:

- experiment creatively with various ways of both making and embellishing fabrics
- develop practical skills by using a new range of tools and materials
- discuss, improve and modify their ideas, and learn about the properties and behaviour of materials
- extend their knowledge of the importance of cloth and textile techniques in other countries and cultures.

ASSESSMENT FOR LEARNING

Assessment is ongoing and is built into each of the sessions. There are regular suggested opportunities for teachers to question and observe pupils during the sessions, each of which includes four practical assessment questions, corresponding to the particular learning objectives set for each session.

Assessment focuses on how children demonstrate new levels of creativity, their growing technical competence in selecting and using appropriate tools for their purpose, or vocabulary to express themselves; their increased critical understanding of their own work and that of their classmates; as well as a broader understanding and sensitivity to the manufacture and use of textiles across history and in different parts of the world. A question for assessment may include, for example: *Can the children say how and why the felt will gradually change?*

> **CD-ROM RESOURCES**
> - Presentations: Felting Masterclass; Batik Masterclass
> - Artworks and images
> - Resource sheets:
>   - Circles
>   - Looms
>   - Weaving a bag
> - Teacher assessment
> - Pupil self-evaluation

SESSION 1 FELTING

LEARNING OBJECTIVES
Children will:

- gain further confidence in their ability to investigate and research by discovering how different fabrics are held together and by experimenting with making felt
- develop their practical skills by using traditional methods, new materials and controlled movements
- learn to predict how the materials will behave and change, and how to modify and manipulate them
- extend their understanding of history and culture by studying how felt is made and used.

VOCABULARY **wool tops**, **weft**, **warp**, **mat** (verb), **fibres**, **kinks**, **friction**

▼ RESOURCES

- ▸ scraps of contemporary manufactured felt
- ▸ woollen garment from charity shop (optional)
- ▸ wool tops (see Suppliers list on the CD-ROM)
- ▸ flat, wipe-clean surfaces
- ▸ jug, hand-hot water (from tap or kettle)
- ▸ washing-up liquid
- ▸ towel (one per child), preferably not too big – pupils can be asked to bring these from home; they will get wet but not damaged
- ▸ sheet of bubble wrap (one per child), slightly smaller than the towel
- ▸ photographic greeting cards, postcards or photographs for stimulus
- ▸ Presentation: Felting Masterclass
- ▸ CD-ROM: images of felt items and felt fibres

ACTIVITY

Begin by giving each group of pupils a piece of modern manufactured felt. Ask them how they think it is made: *Is it woven, knitted or stitched? How is it held together?* Explain that hand-made felt is the oldest form of fabric known in the world. Pieces have been discovered in Turkey dating from 6500BC.

Felt is a soft cloth made by matting together fibres (usually sheep's wool or animal hair) using water and friction. The natural kinks and scales on the hairs catch on each other and hold the structure together. You can demonstrate this by boiling an old woollen garment or putting it through

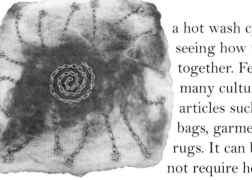

a hot wash cycle and seeing how the fibres mat together. Felt is used in many cultures for making articles such as slippers, bags, garments, tents and rugs. It can be cut but does not require hemming, and is easy to construct by hand (see the images on the CD-ROM).

- The Masterclass shows the basic felting process. Follow this stage by stage. Sometimes, pupils are at first put off by the repetitive actions involved, but speed up with practice. Expect their first piece to be small, with an uneven edge – this is normal.
- Encourage pupils to pull only a small length of wool top from the bag (it must be pulled and teased out gently – it will not respond to tugging!). Ensure that all unused pieces are returned to the bag, or the room will be full of floating wisps!
- When beginning to lay out the wool tops, explain that constructing a piece of felt resembles building up a painting. The first layer of wool tops is the background colour or wash. The second layer deepens or complements this colour. There is no limit to the layers you can add, but three is the bare minimum – any fewer and it will disintegrate. Do not blow, cough or sneeze over the layers or they will blow away! If leaving the room, cover

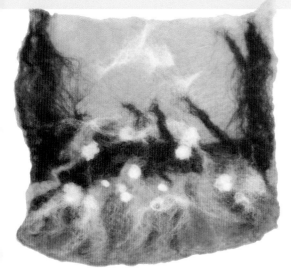

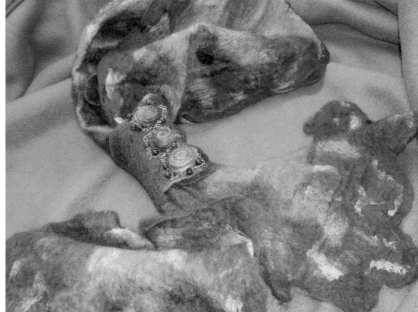

the design gently with a piece of bubble wrap and then a book.

■ By the third layer, the children can position wool tops where they like, as if painting a design on the background colours. They can use a photograph or postcard as inspiration. (The examples shown here are based on the stimulus pictures beside them.)

Recommend that children use only small wisps of wool top – large chunks will separate from the background and come away. Damp felt can be left rolled in a child's towel over a breaktime, lunchtime or overnight – but no longer than this or it will grow mouldy. If left, stick a name label onto each towel roll.

■ When completed, the pieces of felt can be cut, rolled, sewn, manipulated and embellished in whatever way the children wish. Pictured here are a felt purse; felt embroidered in gold chain stitch; a scarf ring (fastened with Velcro) with rolled felt spirals and an old necklace sewn to it; and a scarf with a piece of muslin sandwiched between the layers to give it strength.

■ Finally, gather the class to discuss how they achieved their results and ask them to say what was most successful and why. If time allows, grant a space for thinking and encourage as many children to speak as possible.

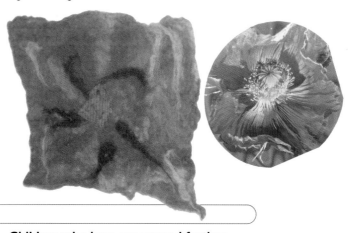

▼ ASSESSMENT FOR LEARNING

Can the children:
▶ construct a piece of felt and explain how it is held together?
▶ control the size of the wool pieces and their position, and roll the towel correctly?
▶ say how the hot water will affect the fibres, and how and why the felt will gradually change?
▶ talk about examples of how felt is and has been used over the centuries?

DIFFERENTIATION

Children who have not progressed as far...
These pupils may need help with pulling out pinches from the wool tops. These should be small and even. Pinch from near the very end, to tease out a wisp that is neither see-through nor dense and chunky.

Children who have progressed further...
Offer these pupils a variety of challenges, such as rolling felt beads; designing a necklace, bag or belt; or making a piece of felt thick enough for oven gloves. They can also experiment with adding other materials to their felting during the construction process.

SESSION 2 FABRIC MANIPULATION – CIRCLES

LEARNING OBJECTIVES
Children will:

- learn to experiment creatively and purposefully by investigating how cloth behaves
- develop practical skills by finding ways of holding and fastening the cloth in the chosen position

- discuss ideas, predict how different cloths will respond and learn to modify their work to achieve their goal
- recognise that cloth is manipulated every day in nearly every culture and country.

VOCABULARY manipulation, swagging, smocking, ruching, names of types of fabric (for example, **taffeta, poplin**) and adjectives to describe them (such as **sheer, dense**)

▼ RESOURCES

- ▶ cloth pieces and scraps in plain colours and varied textures
- ▶ circular embroidery frames
- ▶ fabric scissors
- ▶ needles
- ▶ pins
- ▶ threads
- ▶ beads, sequins, ribbons
- ▶ wadding or stuffing
- ▶ Copydex adhesive
- ▶ named plastic zip bags – good for storing each child's sewing and kit
- ▶ CD-ROM: images of fabric manipulation
- ▶ resource sheet: Circles

ACTIVITY

Introduce the word *manipulate* and invite pupils to describe what it means. It can be both a good thing, such as when an osteopath manipulates joints, or a bad thing, such as when a bully manipulates a person to do what they wish. Ask the children to look up the word in one or more dictionaries. In general, it seems to be defined as 'handling with skill'.

■ What else can be manipulated? Ask pupils to look around the classroom and suggest any materials that have been manipulated, using the **Circles** resource sheet to record their answers. Ideas might include moulded plastics, wood made into tables, metal into window frames, fabric into clothing. Question 2 asks how we are constantly manipulating fabric – such as drawing a curtain, making a bed, pulling clothing into position so it hangs or fits correctly, washing and ironing garments.

■ Refer back to Session 1 of the Textiles unit in *Art Express* Book 5, which gave opportunities for the children to alter fabrics in as many ways as possible. (If you did not follow this session, it would be advantageous to do so before this one; likewise Session 2.) Ask pupils for suggestions for Question 3 – these might include hemming, pleating or stitching. Show the images on the

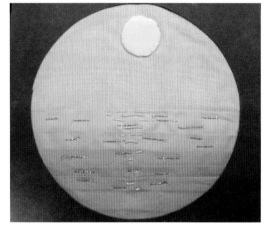

CD-ROM to illustrate many other methods – ruching, swagging, smocking, and so on.

■ Explain that you are taking 'Circles' as a theme, and invite pupils to generate ideas using the resource sheet – roundness, turning movements, rolling, globes, ball shapes, spirals. Provide pieces of cloth, in plain colours only, to show the manipulation techniques clearly, and encourage the children to explore ways in which they could manipulate the cloth to fit the theme. They should discover that different fabrics respond to the same manipulation in different ways, and begin to choose fabrics suitable for different techniques. Challenge pupils to use the cloth in three-dimensional as well as two-dimensional ways.

■ Provide each child with a circular embroidery frame fitted with a background piece of plain cloth. Ask them to record each idea they have, first on the resource sheet and

then by creating it on the background, which will act as their 'sketchbook' or sampler. This is an opportunity for experimenting – so-called 'mistakes' do not matter.

■ When the sampler is complete (see picture, far left on page 50), the children will have a bank of ideas from which to build up a final piece based on circles. This will look best if only one colour range is used, after which suitable embellishments can be added.

Examples shown here, in order of progression, include a small circle of card with thin cloth stretched over and round it to form a moon over the sparkling sea (centre right, page 50); strips of cloth with the raw edges folded in, rolled up tightly and stood up on their ends (below); rolls of cloth laid on their sides and held down by stitches passing right over them (top right); and rolls of cloth that are knotted and held to the background with beads (bottom right). The picture at the very top of page 50 shows

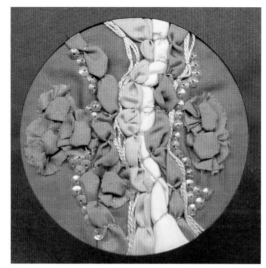

Suffolk puffs – circles of fabric gathered into little bags with a running stitch around the edge, and then stuffed and sewn or stuck onto the background.

■ Finally pair pupils with a 'talking partner' to discuss the work in their samplers, sharing their techniques, triumphs and inspiration, as well as what they might do differently on another occasion. Each pair can then feed back to the rest of the class. Encourage every child to participate.

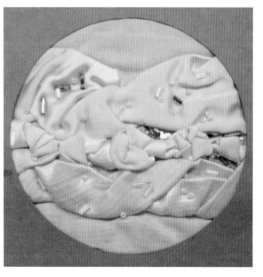

DIFFERENTIATION

Children who have not progressed as far...
By Year 6, it is hoped that most fastenings will be carried out using stitching, but pupils who struggle can carry out manipulation techniques using Copydex adhesive. This should be used in minute amounts so that it lies on, but does not go through, the cloth.

Children who have progressed further...
Challenge these pupils to explore other applications for rolls and spirals (such as a plate of party nibbles) and Suffolk puffs (see Art and Design in Other Areas of Learning on page 58 for further ideas).

SESSION 3 WEAVING ON CARD LOOMS

LEARNING OBJECTIVES

Children will:

■ gain further confidence in their ability to experiment creatively by investigating the use of traditional card looms

■ develop practical skills by manipulating wools and other materials with fingers and weaving needles

■ recognise how a woven fabric is held together and modify the traditional way of doing this

■ extend their understanding of the importance of weaving in nature, culture and history.

VOCABULARY **weave, loom, warp, weft, structure**

▼ RESOURCES

▶ stiff card (greyboard) and equipment for cutting (shape and size will depend on project)
▶ scissors
▶ wools
▶ masking tape (to hold ends of warp thread onto card loom)
▶ weaving needles (large, blunt plastic or metal bodkins)
▶ other materials (such as twigs, ribbon, straw, paper, feathers, leaves)
▶ postcards of views or other subjects
▶ CD-ROM: images of woven items
▶ resource sheets: Looms; Weaving a bag

ACTIVITY

Look at the images on the CD-ROM and ask pupils what they have in common. Once they understand that they are all examples of weaving, ask what they think weaving is for and why it was invented. Compare different examples of woven cloth to test loose weave (such as hessian) against tight weave (for example, cotton or linen). To weave is to form a fabric with interlacing threads, usually on a loom – which is any structure that can be woven on. The interlacing threads are usually vertical (*warp*) and horizontal (*weft*), but not always.

■ Challenge the class to come up with ideas for alternatives to a traditional loom. For example, a loom could be created by hammering nails into the cut end of a log, stretching wool around the nails and weaving among these strands; it could be a twig (see picture, bottom left), a net bag for holding fruit, a bicycle wheel or even a human hand. The **Looms** resource sheet shows some examples.

■ By Year 6, pupils should have already experienced weaving on a card with 'teeth' cut at both ends, and understand that the weaving needle must travel alternately under and over the warp threads. Remind the children of a traditional card loom (see the **Looms** resource sheet for the method, and the box below for tips).

■ Invite pupils to suggest other ways of using card looms. Can they list any possible alterations? These might include the shape of the loom, the direction of warp or weft threads, the materials used for weaving, the method of fastening warp threads, or weaving on both sides of the loom to create a bag (see picture, left) – the **Weaving a bag** resource sheet shows the method for this.

■ The examples shown on these pages are weaving activities that the children can try according to their ability level. They are ranked in order of difficulty, starting with the most easy:

! MAKING CARD LOOMS

▪ Cut 1cm-wide 'teeth' with scissors into the card like a fringe. These are more effective at holding the warp in place than a zigzag edging.
▪ The warp thread must pass only over one side of the card and between the 'teeth', not around the back of the card, or you will not be able to remove the completed weaving.
▪ Always pull the weft thread through the warp so that its end lies in the middle of the loom, not hanging out of the edge.

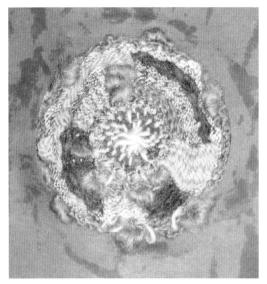

■ Free weaving

The picture at top right of page 52 shows the weft threads passed through the warp in directions other than horizontal. Feathers are incorporated, as well as wools. The finished piece has been mounted on black velvet.

■ Circle weaving

The pictures above, left and right, show weavings made on card circles, where the warp threads have been passed over the front of the card and around the teeth in figure of eight movements. The loom need not be filled and the weft need not go in a spiral (see picture, above right).

■ Weaving over a picture

The picture below right shows a card 'window loom' with small holes pierced in the top and bottom edges through which the loom has been warped up. A postcard has been slotted into place behind it and the child chooses wools to match the picture and weaves over it. For this and for the next idea, it is important to find a picture that lends itself to interpretation through weaving.

■ Weaving to a stimulus

The picture below far right shows a weaving that has been made to follow the design on the central section of a watercolour painting. Note that to achieve the blocks of colour, the weft has been woven only on some warp threads, not right across the loom.

■ Finally, discuss in detail the decisions and suggestions made by pupils. Stimulate the debate with open-ended questions, such as *Why did you think…?*, *What would have happened if…?* that will encourage reasoned answers and higher-order thinking. Allow time for everyone to have a turn at speaking.

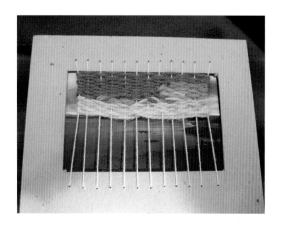

▼ ASSESSMENT FOR LEARNING

Can the children:
▶ show evidence of creative ideas in suggesting different ways to use card looms?
▶ control the warp and weft threads and produce a weaving that holds together?
▶ talk about how a weaving is made and variations they have tried or thought of?
▶ give examples of where weaving is used and where they might find some?

DIFFERENTIATION

Children who have not progressed as far…
Discourage these pupils from pulling too tightly on the weft thread. To help them, rule a vertical red line down each side of the loom where the edges of the weaving should be. If this shows, they are pulling too tightly.

Children who have progressed further…
Challenge these pupils to invent new looms made of card or other materials and create a weaving on them. They could incorporate other materials into the weaving, such as feathers, ribbon, paper, straw, leaves or twigs.

SESSION 4 **BATIK**

LEARNING OBJECTIVES
Children will:

- learn to generate original ideas by responding to a natural form and creating a simple piece of batik
- develop practical skills by learning to control tools, speed and movements

- recognise the properties and behaviour of melted wax on cloth and how this can be harnessed to build a design
- extend their understanding of the history and cultural significance of batik.

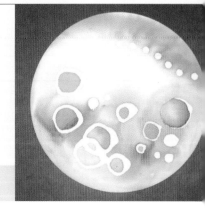

VOCABULARY **batik**, *tjanting*, **wax pot**, **granulated**, **polycotton**

▼ RESOURCES

- ▸ examples of batik
- ▸ electric wax pot
- ▸ wax (granulated is best)
- ▸ old paint brushes
- ▸ scrap paper
- ▸ paper towels
- ▸ *tjanting* brushes
- ▸ plain polycotton cloth
- ▸ circular embroidery frames
- ▸ natural objects (such as pebbles, shells, seedpods or fruit)
- ▸ fabric paints (the examples shown use Brusho)
- ▸ soft paintbrushes, water pots, palettes
- ▸ iron, surface to iron on
- ▸ lots of newspaper
- ▸ Presentation: Batik Masterclass
- ▸ CD-ROM: images of batik

ACTIVITY

Batik (the national art of Indonesia) is a rewarding technique to use with pupils. Ideally, allow a maximum of six children per wax pot and adult. Begin by looking at the images on the CD-ROM and pass around any examples of batik cloth. Next, sit the group around the wax pot to explain the safety rules. Like any hot appliance, the wax pot is safe if used properly. This is because the wax never reaches dangerous temperatures. If some does splash on the skin, it will dry instantly and can be peeled off. Make it a rule that all tools must be *lowered carefully* into the pot, never dropped, and that

there should only ever be one pair of hands at the pot at a time. Place brushes or *tjantings* in the pot with handles pointing out like wheel spokes so a tool can always be reached safely.

- Begin with old paintbrushes and scrap paper. Establishing the correct procedure early is very important; when the children come to use *tjantings*, they will drip continuously.
- Each child needs a 'pad' (paper towel) to protect the non-working hand. The procedure is explained and illustrated step by step in the Presentation: **Batik Masterclass**. If you give each child a number, they can do the procedure in order, the second child starting as soon as the first is away from the pot.
- Repeat the process with the *tjantings*. Let them warm thoroughly and hold them calmly, like a spoonful of milk. If they drip too fast, pinch the spout slightly with pliers. If they drip too slowly, gently insert the point of a pair of compasses to open out the spout.
- When the children are used to the routine, give each one a piece of cloth in a circular frame, and an object for inspiration. Choosing the right stimulus makes a great difference to the results. Natural forms have spots, blobs and uneven qualities, so the inevitable drips of wax add to, rather than spoil, the result. If a child spills wax over a large part of the cloth, you can use this as an experiment – crush

to enhance the spread of colour and chromatography.

■ Iron the batiks between layers of newspaper to remove the wax, changing the paper when it becomes saturated. Two finished and mounted examples are shown here, below and at top right on page 54.

■ When the batiks are complete, give pupils an opportunity to make comparisons between their work and others', to talk about what they have achieved and any difficulties they may have encountered.

at top right on page 54.

the cloth when the wax has dried, and then dye it, allowing the dye to run into the cracks. This crackled effect is a traditional method of batik patterning.

■ Pupils should draw freehand with the *tjanting* directly onto the cloth – avoid pencil, which will be sealed into the cloth. The wax must fully penetrate the cloth, which will turn translucent in these areas. Keep *tjanting* work to a minimum – the more wax you add, the less room for colour. Waxed areas will stay white.

■ Now replace the wax pot, towels and *tjantings* with palettes, water pots, soft brushes and fabric paints. Experiment with these on scrap cloth before painting the batik designs. If using Brusho, paint clean water all over the cloth first and then dot the Brusho on,

▼ ASSESSMENT FOR LEARNING

Can the children:
▸ show evidence of basing their design on a natural form?
▸ use the tools and carry out the technique in a calm, controlled manner?
▸ describe how the wax affects the cloth and the paint, and talk about what they have made?
▸ say where batik comes from and where else it is used in the world?

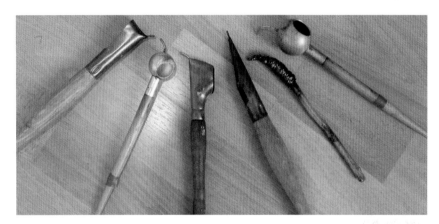

DIFFERENTIATION

Children who have not progressed as far...
Pupils who are not ready to use *tjantings* can still produce a batik using brushes to make the wax design.

Children who have progressed further...
These pupils can progress to adding dyes in layers. After waxing the design onto white cloth, dye the cloth a single colour. Add more wax over this colour and dye in a third colour. When the wax is removed there will be several colours where the child has drawn instead of only white.

SESSION 5 **QUILTED BATIK**

LEARNING OBJECTIVES
Children will:

- learn to select, develop and refine their technical skills and creativity by enhancing their batik pieces with quilting and embellishing
- develop practical skills by learning backstitch and possibly other stitching techniques

- learn to predict how the cloth will respond to the quilting and how tightly the thread is pulled
- extend their understanding of quilting and why and where it is used.

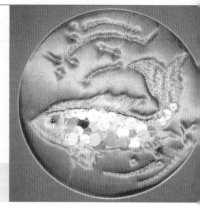

VOCABULARY quilting, embellish, accentuate, enhance, detract, practicality, aesthetics

▼ RESOURCES

- ▶ pieces of manipulated fabric from Session 2
- ▶ batik pieces made in Session 4
- ▶ circular embroidery frames
- ▶ fabric scissors
- ▶ wadding (from a roll, bought by the metre)
- ▶ needles
- ▶ threads
- ▶ beads, sequins
- ▶ CD-ROM: images of quilting and embellishment
- ▶ pupil self-evaluation sheet

ACTIVITY

This session is designed to open pupils' eyes to possibilities for extending and embellishing their batik work, and fabric work in general. They can carry out this process on the batik they made in Session 4, or create a new batik specifically for the purpose. It follows on from Sessions 1 and 2 in the Textiles unit of *Art Express* Book 5, which focus on the alterations that can be made to cloth, and also builds on Session 2 in this book.

■ Look with the class at the examples of fabric manipulation they carried out in Session 2. Ask them to recall ways in which they gave the cloth three-dimensional qualities, such as the Suffolk puff method. Discuss whether these techniques would improve or enhance the batiks made in Session 4.

Ask them to consider whether the manipulation and embellishment techniques used in Session 2 are more striking on plain fabrics, whereas

patterned fabrics plus manipulation techniques could look overpowering and too fussy. Test this theory by ruching a plain and a highly patterned drape. The ruching may enhance the qualities, texture and shadows of a plain fabric such as silk or velvet, but detract from the pattern in the other cloth and be too 'busy'. Suggest that pupils' batiks should be enhanced only with very subtle methods.

■ To quilt batik, place the inner ring of an embroidery frame on a surface (see picture, bottom left). Cover this with a piece of thin cloth – any scrap cloth will do, as this will not show (bottom centre). Over this, lay a piece of wadding (bottom right). Over the wadding, place the ironed batik. Finally unscrew the outer ring of the embroidery frame until it is quite wide, and push it over the layers before screwing it up tightly and trimming to a 2cm frill (page 57, bottom right).

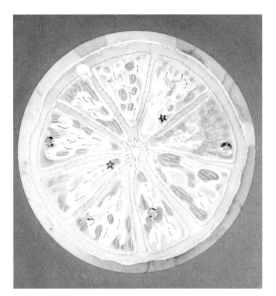

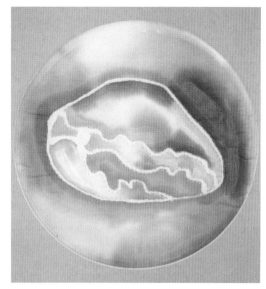

The thicker the wadding, the more accentuated the quilting effect will be when you stitch through it. If the layers are too thick to sandwich into the embroidery frame, they can be held together with pins, but this makes them less easy to quilt.

■ When quilting, select lines to stitch along or areas to surround with stitching (see picture above, which shows a batik based on a halved orange). The neater and closer the stitching, the more pronounced the three-dimensional qualities will be. The picture at top right shows a batik based on a pebble that has been quilted with double lines of back-stitching in four different toning colours of thread. As with batik, quilting calls for simple lines to produce maximum effect.

■ Small single stitches, sequins or beads can be pulled in tightly to produce a dimple in the fabric. In the picture at top left, metallic thread has been used to suggest a juicy sparkle and sequins act as seeds.

■ The images on the CD-ROM show other examples of quilting and embellishment. Can pupils see that quilting can be used for both practical and aesthetic reasons, and how the two might combine, for example on an eiderdown or quilted jacket?

■ Discuss the unit work in detail, starting with content and moving on to composition and other qualities. Ask open-ended *What do you think…?* questions to inspire higher-order thinking, and encourage everyone to have a turn at speaking. You can give the class copies of the **Pupil self-evaluation** sheet to record their progress.

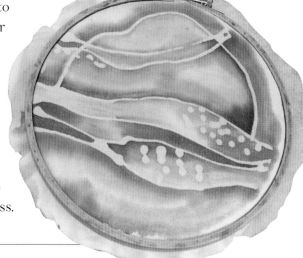

▼ ASSESSMENT FOR LEARNING

Can the children:
▸ show evidence of technical skills when carrying out quilting and embellishing on their batik?
▸ control the needle and thread to carry out backstitch or other embroidery stitches?
▸ explain how the cloth responds to the quilting technique?
▸ understand why and where quilting is used and how practicality and aesthetics can be combined?

DIFFERENTIATION

Children who have not progressed as far…
Pupils whose stitching skills are less developed can add simple or random stitches to quilted pieces for embellishment, which will still produce a dimpled three-dimensional effect. Ideally, they should be taught backstitch on a large scale using Binca fabric or similar. Once the method is grasped, the children can then quilt their batik piece.

Children who have progressed further…
These pupils can be offered quilting challenges, such as stitching along both sides of a waxed line (as in the pebble shown at the top of this column) or embellishing using other stitches, such as chain stitch or French knots.

OTHER AREAS OF LEARNING

LITERACY

- Children can study the role of textiles in stories, such as the theme of spinning, weaving or sewing in many traditional fairytales.
- Ask children to consider the phrases *spinning a yarn*, *weaving a tale*, *following the thread*, *a tapestry of lies* and the word *spinster*.

SCIENCE

- Pupils can research how cloth was dyed in ancient times. They could try natural dyeing with plants and compare this method with those used today.
- Children could test different materials and review their findings to ascertain their suitability as insulating materials.

MATHEMATICS

- Weaving, spinning, knitting and stitching are all based on counting, rhythms and sequences. Ask children to design a symmetrical pattern for a woven rug on finely squared paper.
- Pupils could investigate the importance of measurements in textiles and clothing.
- Can children use number sequencing and regular shapes to design a patterned fabric?

Textiles

ART AND DESIGN

- Waterfall: ask each child to make several Suffolk puffs from plain, stone-coloured fabrics stuffed with newspaper. Pin to a long vertical wall, poke tufts of green wool between for plants, and hang a sheer blue-green chiffon scarf from the top to hang loosely over the 'stones'.
- Spacescape: ask pupils to make large Suffolk puffs (draw around a dustbin lid) from grey/black/silver cloths. Add silver sequins. Display on a black background.

GEOGRAPHY

- Ask the class to compare cloths made and worn in Britain with traditional cloth from other countries and cultures, such as India, China, Ghana and Peru. Can they find out the meaning behind the designs and how they are constructed?

MUSIC

- Women used to sing songs to the rhythm of the spinning wheel or weaving shuttle. Why might they have done this? Ask pupils to find examples of folk songs of this type and try composing their own rhythmic verses or accompaniment.

HISTORY

- Ask children to research felt, the world's oldest fabric, and early clothing, finding out how much work was involved in making one garment, such as a woollen cloak.
- Pupils could look at examples of wills leaving clothing to family members, and compare this with today's throwaway society.
- Request children to find out the history of the Bayeux Tapestry.
- Children can compare looms throughout history, such as Victorian hand and steam looms and Aztec back-strap looms.

Sculptures of the human figure have been created in many different ways. In early times, figures were carved from natural materials, such as wood, stone and rock, and were often used as symbols in religious ceremonies. Later, casting techniques were used. Shapes of figures were modelled in clay, then a cast of the clay shapes would be made in plaster. Finally, the cast would be filled with bronze or other metals. In more recent times, sculptors have constructed figures from found materials and then cast them in more permanent materials such as bronze. Some sculptors, including Giacometti, have created figures by modelling form onto an armature (a wire or wood framework) with clay or plaster.

Prior to Year 6, children will have developed ideas for their sculpture by transforming their two-dimensional designs into three-dimensional structures. They will have applied and refined construction techniques to express their own ideas, evaluating and modifying work to suit their intentions. They will have broadened their experience of sculpture and developed an understanding of the thinking processes that sculptors use to produce abstract sculpture.

Over the course of this unit, children will explore the moving figure as a starting point for making a sculpture. They will look at how the idea of movement is shown by sculptors, both contemporary and in the past. Pupils will develop modelling and construction skills using wire and plaster-impregnated bandage to make a sculpture of a figure in motion. They will construct an initial armature from wire, and then build up the form of muscles. Finally, they will model form and details using plaster-impregnated bandage. The children will adapt their work as necessary, describing how they might develop it further, using appropriate technical vocabulary.

AIMS

This unit offers pupils the opportunity to:

- explore and develop ideas about movement by selecting information from visual research
- apply their knowledge and understanding of materials and processes, selecting, combining and manipulating them to explore the visual and tactile qualities
- evaluate and critically review their work, identifying both successful aspects and others needing further development, adapting and improving their own work as it progresses
- develop knowledge and understanding by comparing ideas, methods and approaches used by different sculptors, relating this to the time and place in which the work was made, using appropriate specialist vocabulary.

ASSESSMENT FOR LEARNING

Throughout the sessions presented in the unit, continually assess children's ability to confidently collect and select information from visual research. By the end of the unit, you should look for specific evidence to show that the children have developed construction and modelling skills to make a sculpture that communicates their ideas about movement. Assess the children's levels of knowledge and understanding of sculpture, together with their individual ability to adapt and improve their work to realise their own ideas.

▶ **CD-ROM RESOURCES**

- Presentation: Constructing and modelling a figure Masterclass
- Images and artworks
- Resource sheets:
  - Sculptures of figures in motion (1–4)
  - Analysing sculpture–figures in motion
  - Sculpture terms
- Teacher assessment
- Pupil self-evaluation

SESSION 1 | **THE FIGURE IN MOTION**

LEARNING OBJECTIVES

Children will:

- learn to develop their ideas purposefully by selecting visual information about a figure in motion, from direct observation
- develop their ability to observe and record by selecting and recording the form, line, shape

and pattern of a figure from different viewpoints

- develop the ability to collect visual research about colour through the use of colour notes in their sketchbooks.

VOCABULARY line, shape, texture, pattern, form, space, pose, position, gesture, open/closed shape, proportion, balance, action, repetition, sequence, dynamic, flowing, motion, rhythm, forceful, expressive, boundary, contour, edge, outline, profile

▼ RESOURCES

- ▶ sports equipment, for example, hockey sticks, cricket bats, footballs, javelins, tennis racquets, discuses, hula-hoops
- ▶ 2B and 4B pencils
- ▶ A2 cartridge paper
- ▶ sketchbooks
- ▶ soft coloured pencils
- ▶ digital camera, if available
- ▶ CD-ROM: images of figures in motion

ACTIVITY

In this session, children will explore activities such as sport or dance as a starting point for making work in three dimensions. The children will draw a figure from four different angles – the front, back and both sides – from direct observation. Through drawing, the children will be finding out and learning about the structure of the body. These drawings will give them information about the figure 'in the round' and will be used as a basis for their sculpture. Provide children with a variety of sports equipment. The class will need to work in a large area, such as a school hall, in order to view the whole figure at a distance.

■ Explain to the children that the purpose of the session is to collect information about a figure in motion. The drawings will be used for information when making their sculpture. (See the images of figures in motion on the CD-ROM.)

■ Put the children into pairs and ask each pair to choose a sport related to the equipment available (for example, tennis, basketball, netball, football), or you could allocate the sports, to ensure a wide variety of sports is represented.

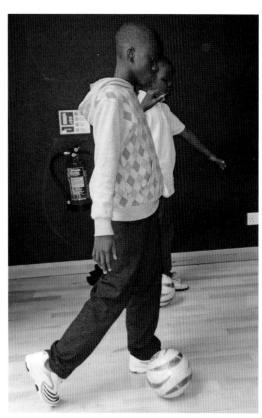

Ask pupils to rehearse body gesture and movement. Challenge them to imagine various action sequences in 'slow motion', such as sprinting from a start line or throwing a discus. Discuss the joints in the body. Make sure the children follow the action through – this will give them a feeling of transference of weight and balance.

■ Ask one of each pair to strike a pose that describes an action, then invite the other child to draw the figure from different viewpoints – front, sides and back view. Guide them as to where in the hall they should pose and check that the person drawing is far enough away to see the whole figure. Inform the class that they will have about ten minutes for each pose. After the first child has finished all four drawings, ask the pairs to swap roles. Provide A2 cartridge paper and explain to the children that they are to use the paper in a landscape position so they can draw the four figures side by side on the paper. Explain that if they look

carefully, they will notice more and want to change parts of their drawing. Encourage them to work over the top of their initial light sketches. Deter children from using rubbers.

■ Advise the children to draw what they see, rather than what they know. For some children you will need to ask questions to focus their looking, while other children may have advanced to the stage where they pose their own questions as they draw. Do not give the children a ready formula for drawing a figure; they will progress naturally and develop confidence through careful observation.

■ When both children in each pair have finished their drawings, ask them to draw the figure again quickly in their sketchbooks and make colour notes using coloured pencils. This information will be used when the children paint their sculptures of figures in motion in Session 5.

■ Take a photograph of each figure from different viewpoints using a digital camera, if available; these may be used to supplement the drawings.

TEACHING POINT

Pupils will work at their own stage of development; accept whatever they draw. By focusing children's looking through careful questioning, they will make progress faster. In Year 6, if children have already developed observational skills, they will be asking their own internal questions as they draw, for example: *How does the arm join onto the shoulder?*

▼ ASSESSMENT FOR
  LEARNING

Can the children:
▸ produce well observed drawings, using strong lines to show movement?
▸ confidently collect visual research by making colour notes in their sketchbooks within the set time limit?

DIFFERENTIATION

Children who have not progressed as far…
Some pupils may need a teacher to focus their looking, for example: *Can you see the whole arm? Only draw the part you can see.* If the children have difficulty filling the whole space on the paper, ask them to draw the outline with their finger before using the pencil.

Children who have progressed further…
If possible, provide a skeleton for these pupils to draw. Ask them to look at how the body is supported and make connections with their drawings. Extend the children's understanding by careful questioning to analyse the action, weight and balance of the figure.

SESSION 2 **TECHNIQUES USING WIRE**

LEARNING OBJECTIVES
Children will:

- develop practical skills by exploring and experimenting with wire to develop basic techniques and control of tools
- learn about sculpture by considering the context in which sculptors worked
- learn to compare and comment on the ideas, methods and approaches of other sculptors.

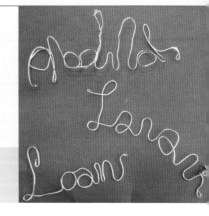

VOCABULARY linear, transform, depict, figurative, abstract, realistic, representational, proportion, balance, casting, carving, solid, hollow, scale, form, mass, space, shape

▼ RESOURCES

- ▸ modelling wire (1.25mm) or soft aluminium rod (2mm)
- ▸ pliers – snipe-nosed pliers, combination pliers and side-cutters
- ▸ reproductions of sculptures showing figures in motion
- ▸ CD-ROM:
  images of Alexander Calder's work;
  images of sculptures showing figures in motion
- ▸ resource sheets:
  Sculpture of figures in motion (1–4);
  Analysing sculpture – figures in motion;
  Sculpture terms

ACTIVITY

In the first part of the session, pupils will experiment with wire in order to practise their techniques. In the second half, they will look at sculpture from different eras that portrays movement. The two different parts may be taught separately. Prepare the wire in advance by cutting a variety of lengths, and bending the ends over with pliers.

- Start the session by clarifying health and safety issues, and explain the reason for bending the ends of the wire. Next, show the class pliers with different shaped ends. Show that the long-nosed (snipe-nosed) pliers are for bending the wire, the flat-ended (combination) pliers are for squashing the wire, and the sharp-edged (side-cutter) pliers are for cutting. Show how to cut the wire safely.

- Explain to the children that the aim of the activity is to draw their name from a continuous length of wire, using their fingers and pliers to bend the wire. Encourage the children to persevere.

- As a plenary, discuss with the class the challenges they encountered with the springy nature of the wire and how they overcame them.

- Project an image of the work of Alexander Calder (see the CD-ROM) onto the interactive whiteboard and ask pupils to make connections with their own work. Introduce the idea of drawing with wire.

- To begin the second part of the session, project the **Sculpture of figures in motion** resource sheet onto the interactive whiteboard. Invite the class to look at the images of sculptures. Initially, they could work in pairs to match each sculpture with the relevant information. Initiate a class discussion where the children must give reasons for their answers. Focus the debate on the following questions: *What materials were the sculptures made from? Why were the sculptures made from these materials?* Talk with pupils about how the sculptures were made and introduce the method of *casting*. Explain how the sculptor models the main forms of the figure in clay and then makes a cast of the forms in plaster. The cast is then filled with

! TEACHING TIP

If possible, organise a visit to a sculpture park, museum or gallery to enable the children to have direct experience of figurative sculpture 'in the round'.

bronze. Focus the children's attention on the Roman copy of the ancient Greek sculpture. Ask them to consider how the sculptor carved the figure from marble. What tools would the sculptor use? Ask them to bear in mind when the sculptures were made.

■ Question pupils as to why they think the ancient Greeks made sculptures of athletes. Talk about how they were expressing their idealised portrait of an athlete through sculpting a perfectly proportioned body.

■ Divide the class into groups of four or five children. Give each group a reproduction of a sculpture from the **Sculpture of figures in motion** resource sheets 1 and 2, or one of the images from the CD-ROM. Within their groups, ask the children to talk through the following areas: content, form, process and mood of their sculpture (you can project the

Analysing sculpture – figures in motion resource sheet onto the whiteboard to stimulate discussion). Ask each group to give a presentation to the rest of the class.

■ Organise the class into groups, and give each group one of the sets of words from the **Sculpture terms** resource sheet. Ask them to look up their three terms in a dictionary or thesaurus. These can be copied into their sketchbooks for reference. You may wish to add the definitions to a classroom display.

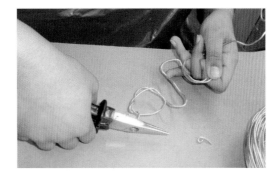

Can the children:
▶ explore the visual and tactile qualities of wire, and confidently use basic techniques and tools safely?
▶ comment on the context in which some sculptors worked?
▶ use an increasing vocabulary relating to sculpture and three-dimensional materials to compare different methods and approaches used by sculptors?

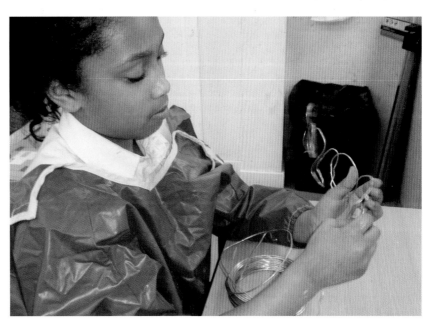

DIFFERENTIATION

Children who have not progressed as far...
Ask these pupils to write their names using joined-up letters on paper to give them a concrete example and help them follow the shapes of the letters. Give support to children with fine motor skills difficulties. In discussions, provide a good language role model for children with English as an additional language.

Children who have progressed further...
Ask these pupils to draw a self-portrait or a portrait of a friend using a continuous line. Then invite them to translate the design using wire to draw the face. Encourage them to look up the more unusual sculpture terms. They can also look at the work of Alexander Calder who used wire to draw faces.

SESSION 3 **CONSTRUCTING AN ARMATURE**

LEARNING OBJECTIVES
Children will:
- learn to express and develop ideas by using visual research to create a sculpture of a figure in motion
- develop technical skills by constructing an armature of a figure from wire
- develop their knowledge and understanding of materials and processes by selecting, combining and manipulating them to explore line, structure, space, form and balance.

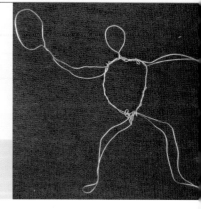

VOCABULARY line, tone, shape, texture, colour, pattern, form, space, armature, balance, pose, position, outline, open/closed shape, expressive, construct, profile

▼ RESOURCES

- ▸ drawings from Session 1
- ▸ modelling wire (1.25mm) or soft aluminium rod (2mm)
- ▸ pliers – snipe-nosed pliers, combination pliers and side-cutters
- ▸ wooden base, 2cm thick, 16cm x 16cm (use offcuts or chipboard)
- ▸ wall stapler
- ▸ wooden bases
- ▸ telephone wire or fuse wire (for racquet)
- ▸ Presentation: Constructing and modelling a figure Masterclass

ACTIVITY

In this session, pupils will construct an armature for their sculpture. Ensure they have adequate space to work. It will take the children time to make the armature; encourage them to persevere if they encounter problems. Prior to the session, cut the wire to varying lengths – one long piece, 120–125cm, to make the head, torso and legs, and a shorter length of 80cm for the arms. It is easier to work from long lengths of wire, as it is difficult to join wire and the join is always weak. The height of the armature should be about 30cm.

- At the beginning of the session, hand out the children's drawings from Session 1. Explain to pupils that they will need to refer to their drawings for the basic lines, shapes and form of the

figure. Remind them to work 'in the round', looking at each drawing from different viewpoints.

- Ask the children to make the pose in their drawings, and think about the position of their feet. Point out that the feet need to be apart in order to give greater balance and stability to the body. Next, ask pupils to think about the joints in their bodies – where are they? In what direction can they move? Ask them to think about the position of the joints – the elbow, knee, wrist, and ankle.

- Demonstrate how to make a simple armature (see the Masterclass). In the middle of the length of wire, make a circular head and twist the wire to make the neck. Then form a round body shape (a larger circle) and twist the wire. You will have a length of wire each side of the body. Double up the wire to make a leg. Model the foot, then twist the end of the wire (about 3–4cm) into the body shape; bend it to make the knee. Use the double thickness to model the shape of muscles. Repeat for the other leg. Model the shape of the shoulders from the circular body.

- Allow time for pupils to work at their own pace to construct the head, body and legs. At this point, ask the children to look carefully at their drawings, focusing on the shape of the tennis racquet, hockey stick and so on.

Can the children:
▸ select relevant information about the figure in motion from their drawings, with an awareness of balance and proportion, and work purposefully to realise their ideas?
▸ apply skills and techniques using wire to make an armature from visual research, independently or with support?
▸ manipulate the visual qualities to suit their intentions?

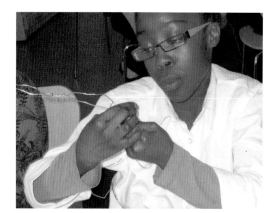

■ Double up the wire to construct the hockey stick and arm. Join the end of the wire to the shoulders by twisting. Shape the hands. Bend the wire to make the elbow and wrist joints.

■ Ask pupils to refer to their sketches to model movement in the figure. They need to consider the joints in the body, bending the wire appropriately.

■ Finally, when pupils have constructed their armature, use a wall stapler to staple the feet to a wooden block (adults only). Make sure the feet are some distance apart so that the figure balances. The hockey stick can also be stapled to the base for added stability. Thin wire can be used to make the strings of the tennis racquet.

■ Use the shorter piece of wire for the arms. If the figure is holding a hockey stick or tennis racquet, the wire will need to be longer as the arm and hockey stick will be made from one piece of wire. To construct the arms, thread the middle of the piece of wire through the back of the body shape (the shoulders) and twist to secure.

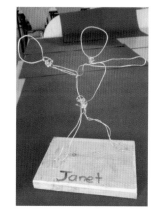

DIFFERENTIATION

Children who have not progressed as far...
Pupils with poor fine motor skills will need individual adult support when making their armature. Some may need help with proportions – if the body or head is too big, the armature will topple over. Remind the children about joints, especially the bent knees – this will make the armature more stable.

Children who have progressed further...
Ask these pupils to consider the shapes of the muscles in the arms and legs on their armature. Can they make the outline of the hand accurately? Stimulate them to think of alternative means of making strings for the tennis racquet (for example, using fuse wire or telephone wire).

SESSION 4 MODELLING FORM

LEARNING OBJECTIVES
Children will:
- learn to create and develop ideas by exploring and combining the visual qualities of form and space using modelling techniques
- develop and refine their modelling skills by using newspaper and plaster-impregnated bandage to build up form
- learn to reflect and refine their work as it develops.

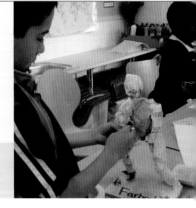

VOCABULARY **line, shape, texture, pattern, form, space, construct, model, underlying structure, mass, plane, armature**

▼ RESOURCES

- ▸ drawings and photographs from Session 1
- ▸ armatures from Session 3
- ▸ newspaper
- ▸ masking tape
- ▸ sugar paper to cover tables
- ▸ scissors
- ▸ plaster-impregnated bandage (Mod Roc)
- ▸ containers for cut strips
- ▸ stable water pots
- ▸ protective clothing

! HEALTH & SAFETY

Plaster dust is a health hazard. Use a damp cloth to wipe surfaces regularly. If weather permits, carry out this session in the playground or on the school field to reduce the dust problem. There will be less cleaning up!

ACTIVITY

In this session, pupils will be modelling the form of muscles onto the wire armature using newspaper. They will then use plaster-impregnated bandage to model form and refine details. The two parts of the session may be taught separately.

■ Explain to the children that they are to work from their drawings from Session 1. Tape the drawings and photographs onto the wall where each child can see theirs easily.

MODELLING THE FORM OF MUSCLES USING NEWSPAPER

Demonstrate how to make the head by crushing newspaper into a ball. Model it into the shape of the head and cover it with more newspaper. Push the ball into the circle of wire for the head and attach it to the armature with short pieces of masking tape. Ask pupils to make a larger ball of newspaper for the body, flattening it into the shape of the body and shoulders. Attach it securely with masking tape. Remind the class not to bandage the body with too much masking tape.

■ Ask the children to look at the muscles in their forearm. Can they describe the shape of the muscle? Then ask them to compare the size of their wrist to the size of the muscle in their forearm. Which side of the arm is the muscle attached to? Then focus on the biceps. How does the shape of the

muscle change when they move their arm? Look at the muscles in the thigh and the calf. Where are they attached on the leg?

■ Demonstrate how to model the form of the forearm muscles by moulding newspaper. Remind pupils that the muscle needs to be thinner at the wrist end. Model the biceps muscle and tape it onto the armature. Again, deter the children from bandaging the armature with paper.

■ Model the form of the muscles in the legs in the same way. Model the feet with small pads of newspaper. Make a small pad of newspaper for the bottom and attach it with tape.

MODELLING FORM USING PLASTER-IMPREGNATED BANDAGE

Cover the tables with old sheets of sugar paper. Provide each child with a stable water pot. Supply trays for the cut strips of bandage.

■ Ask pupils to cut the Mod Roc into strips about 1.5cm wide and 8cm long.

Can the children:
▸ combine and organise
  the visual qualities
  appropriately to suit
  their intentions?
▸ use plaster-impregnated
  bandage effectively
  to model form and
  detail based on their
  observational drawings
  and photographs?
▸ adapt their work as
  needed and describe
  how they might develop
  it further?

Show them how to pull the strip of Mod Roc through the water, press it around the form, then smooth it down with a finger. Start modelling the legs and feet first as this will make the armature more stable. Encourage the children to work from their drawings, turning the armature to view the figure from different angles as they build up the form.

■ Encourage pupils to review their work during the making process.

■ Cut some thinner, shorter pieces for the neck and face. When covering the neck, take care not to make it too thick. The children can model the features on the face with the Mod Roc. The form of the hair can be made from twisted thin strips. Hands can be carefully modelled from smaller strips. The clothing for the figure can be made from wider strips.

DIFFERENTIATION

Children who have not progressed as far...
Pupils with limited fine motor skills may need adult support and an individual demonstration to understand how to model muscles. A wooden articulated model of a figure would show the form and position of muscles clearly.

Children who have progressed further...
Challenge these pupils by encouraging them to model and refine details of features on the face and hands. Motivate them to model details of clothing, such as collars and cuffs. They may require extra time to make their sculpture.

SESSION 5 PAINTING FIGURES, REVIEWING AND EVALUATING

LEARNING OBJECTIVES
Children will:

- further develop their practical skills by applying colour to their sculpture, working from their colour notes
- learn to look critically by considering the work they have done and identifying both successful aspects and others that might need further development
- develop knowledge and understanding by considering the work and methods of other sculptors.

VOCABULARY **line**, **tone**, **shape**, **texture**, **colour**, **pattern**, **form**, **space**, **rhythm**, **movement**, **balance**, **sculpture**, **construct**, **model**, **proportion**, **viewpoint**, **structure**, **armature**

▼ RESOURCES

- ▸ drawings and photographs from Session I
- ▸ sketchbook colour notes from Session I
- ▸ sculptures of figures from Session 4
- ▸ acrylic or ready-mixed paint in the double primary colour system
- ▸ medium hog-hair brushes, size 10 and 12
- ▸ fine brushes, size 6 and 8
- ▸ mixing palettes for ready-mixed paint or A4 white sugar paper for mixing acrylic paint
- ▸ water pots
- ▸ A4 white sugar paper for testing colours
- ▸ protective clothing
- ▸ pupil self-evaluation sheet

ACTIVITY

During this session, pupils will be painting their sculptures using their colour notes made in Session 1. It is advisable to paint the sculptures using acrylic paint as it will dry with a slightly shiny finish. The paint can be dispensed onto an A4 sheet of white sugar paper; another A4 sheet can be used as a mixing palette, which can be thrown away at the end of the session. Each child will need their own water pot, brushes and mixing sheet; the palette of colours can be shared between two pupils. If acrylic paint is not available, ready-mixed paint can be used instead.

During the second part of the session, the children will evaluate their own work and that of their classmates, and make links with the work of professional artists. You may wish to teach the session in two parts.

- Explain to the class that they are to paint their sculptures referring to their colour notes, backed up by photographs, to give them information about colour. During a group discussion, ask the children to describe the sequence of colour mixing. Discuss points to remember when painting their sculptures, for example: that it is important to wash their brushes well to ensure clear colours; and to select the right size and type of brush to paint broader or smaller areas.

- Begin by mixing and matching skin tones. Identify areas to paint, such as the hands, arms, neck and face. Ask, *What do you notice happens to the paint?* As the plaster is absorbent, they may have to apply two coats of the paint for good coverage.

- The torso can be painted next, and then the legs and feet. When the paint is dry, ask pupils to select the right-sized brush to add details onto the clothing, such as stripes on a tracksuit or details on trainers. At this point, the children can also paint the features on the face. Ask them to think about the colours needed for different parts of the eye. Can they describe the shape and colour of the lips? Mix the colour of eyebrows; hair can be painted at the same time. Before painting the base, ask pupils to select a colour for the surface their sport would be played on (for example, grass or sand).

■ Gather the class together and talk about the techniques they have used: constructing the armature with wire; modelling form with newspaper; and modelling with plaster-impregnated bandage. What did they learn about the materials they used?

■ For a final evaluation, ask the class to discuss the following questions with a partner or 'critical friend': *Do you think your sculpture expresses a real feeling of movement? How? How well do you think you achieved your intentions? What did you find most challenging during the process of making? How did you resolve these difficulties? Which parts are you most pleased with? Why? Can you suggest three ways in which your partner's sculpture is successful and three ways in which your partner could improve their work? Can you name any sculptors who have used similar techniques for their work?*

Finally, you can distribute copies of the **Pupil self-evaluation** sheet for the children to complete.

▼ ASSESSMENT FOR LEARNING

Can the children:
▶ work with care to apply colour accurately to their sculpture, refining it by adding details?
▶ critically review their work, clearly identifying successful aspects and areas to improve?
▶ make comments that demonstrate knowledge and understanding about other sculptors' ways of working?

DIFFERENTIATION

Children who have not progressed as far...
Before painting details, these pupils can experiment with painting fine lines on a test sheet. They may need more water to make the paint free flowing. If they struggle to make skin tones, ask others to offer basic ingredients. To develop confidence, encourage these children also to help others make colours.

Children who have progressed further...
These pupils may need more time to add details to their sculpture. Ask them to research sculptors (such as Elizabeth Frink, Rodin, Michelangelo or Antony Gormley) and give a short presentation about their work. They could make a timeline of sculptors to be added to a class display.

OTHER AREAS OF LEARNING

HISTORY

- Understanding the importance of sport in ancient Greek society would help pupils develop a deeper appreciation of Greek sculpture. They could research the origins of the Olympic Games and produce a report on the Greek legacy in the modern Olympics, including an assessment of their different sources of information.
- Studying Greek sculptures on the internet or in museums and galleries helps children learn about proportion and balance in the human figure.

LITERACY

- While looking at figurative sculpture (ideally through first-hand experience, in the environment or in a museum or gallery), the class could consider how they would write a description of the sculpture for a blind person. Pupils can discuss their ideas with a partner, thinking about scale and the materials the sculpture is made from. They could make analogies and use metaphors and similes.

Sculpture

ICT

- The class could create a multimedia presentation about making their sculptures. They could use digital photographs and video clips, and include information about professional sculptors and how they develop their ideas.

PHYSICAL, SOCIAL AND HEALTH EDUCATION (PSHE)

- Pupils can explore movement patterns in dance, gymnastics and sports activities. They can explore actions and shapes through twisting, turning and balancing. They will develop skills in athletic activities such as running, jumping, throwing and catching a ball.
- Children could choose a dance or gymnastics movement as a starting point for their figurative sculpture.
- A link can be made with 'Keeping healthy'. Pupils can research how we need exercise to stay healthy and maintain our muscles.

SCIENCE

Links can be made with 'Moving and growing'.
Pupils can:
- learn about the structure of the skeleton
- learn how the skeleton supports the body
- identify bones
- notice how muscles are attached to bones
- observe the body's joints and how they move
- look at the body's muscles, investigating how they contract and relax
- apply their observations of the skeleton, how the body moves and the position and movement of the muscles when making their figurative sculptures.

Using computers in art and design can make a significant contribution to pupils' creativity by providing another tool for them to extend and develop creative ideas. ICT can be used:

■ as a starting point for the research and development of ideas – to create or select appropriate primary and secondary resources

■ as an intermediate stage in the art and design process – to manipulate primary and secondary resource materials on screen in order to plan work in more traditional media

■ as a final stage – to create a finished piece of work in printed form, or in electronic form as a single image, document, animated sequence or multimedia presentation.

Unlike work executed in traditional materials, there are no precedents for using digital media in primary schools. New technologies are without doubt part of the landscape of a modern child's daily experience. ICT should be viewed as a creative tool and pupils provided with plentiful opportunities to experiment, make mistakes and explore its potential. To view ICT as a tool merely to replicate what can already be achieved using traditional media, denies its enormous potential.

Prior to Year 6, children will have had the experience of manipulating images in different ways and will have gained confidence in using software with layers to make creative images.

In this unit, pupils will use digital media to combine simple costume construction with layers to make a statement on a theme. They will also study the work of an artist who uses both traditional and digital processes. Sessions 1 and 2 should be taught together, as should Sessions 3, 4 and 5.

To complete the work in this unit, you will require image-manipulation software that has layers, such as *Photoshop Elements* – a relatively inexpensive yet powerful software

package. You can download a trial version from the Adobe website at www.adobe.com/uk.

AIMS

This unit offers pupils the opportunity to:

■ combine digital and traditional techniques

■ further develop image-manipulation skills, designing for a purpose

■ develop an understanding of the creative potential of digital technology

■ use their understanding to refine, develop, adapt and discuss their own work.

ASSESSMENT FOR LEARNING

This unit enables pupils to practise their skills and develop ideas using their imagination. Some of the creative ideas are developed on screen from digital photographs, while others require the use of traditional materials to create collages or costumes that are then photographed for further work on screen. Look for growing confidence in the ways that children use and select tools for a specific purpose. Question them about how those tools can be used to create particular effects. Look also for evidence of pupils' developing understanding in choosing tools for modifying and cutting from varied types of image. Can they use different cutting tools to select all or parts of an image? Can they use filters to change the mood of an image through effective choice of colour and transparency?

▶ **CD-ROM RESOURCES**
■ Presentation: Responding to artists; *Photoshop Elements*: Text and page layout Masterclass
■ Artworks and images
■ Resource sheets:
  ■ Framework for looking
  ■ Making the structure
  ■ Using Lazertran (1–4)
  ■ Costume construction techniques
  ■ Page layout
■ Teacher assessment
■ Pupil self-evaluation

SESSION 1 **SELF-IMAGE**

LEARNING OBJECTIVES

Children will:

- develop and refine their skills and understanding of techniques by creating a portrait image of themselves using photographs of self, family, friends, maps and objects

- learn how art can express ideas by considering the work of an artist who uses digital media.

VOCABULARY self-image, collage, layer, filter

▼ RESOURCES

- ▸ computer
- ▸ image-manipulation software (such as *Photoshop Elements*)
- ▸ photographs of self, family, house, map and favourite object
- ▸ Presentation: Responding to artists
- ▸ resource sheet: Framework for looking

ACTIVITY

In this session and the next, pupils will create a layered self-image on the computer and then work with the printouts or transfers to create a collage on a strip of wood. The wooden sections will then be assembled to create a group portrait.

In preparation for this session, ask the children to collect the following resources: photographs of themselves, their family and their house, a map of where they live and a favourite object. Alternatively, they could collect images of the time they have spent at the

school and develop this into a mixed-media piece. Photograph or scan the children's collections in advance and store them in a shared area on the computer network.

Also in preparation, look at the work of Paul Clifford on the internet (paulclifford.net/home.html). Look in particular at the Hidden Rivers project and at the different ways the images are layered together.

■ Gather the class together and use the interactive whiteboard to show them the work of Paul Clifford. Explain that the artist creates his pieces by combining fragments from different images to create new personal statements, combining both digitally manipulated imagery and paint. After creating his initial digital image, Clifford often uses a transfer process to apply it to a canvas or board.

Give pupils copies of the **Framework for looking** resource sheet to use as a discussion model when investigating this artist's work. (The resource sheet is based on the Presentation: **Responding to artists**.) Explain to the children that they will use similar techniques to Clifford's to create their own self-image.

■ Clarify to the class that the term *self-image* is used here to describe different aspects of a person and not a self-portrait, which usually means solely a visual image of oneself.

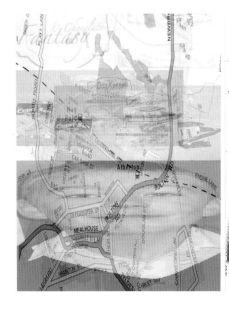

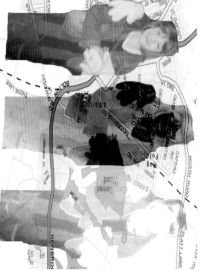

! SAVING IMAGES

When you create a layered image in Photoshop and save it, the extension .psd is added to the file name (for example, image1.psd). This is the Photoshop default setting and means that all the layers are preserved. If you intend to work on the image again, you must use this format. If the *Photoshop* image is saved as a .jpg file, the layers will be lost as this format does not support layers. Only flatten and save as a .jpg when the work is completed.

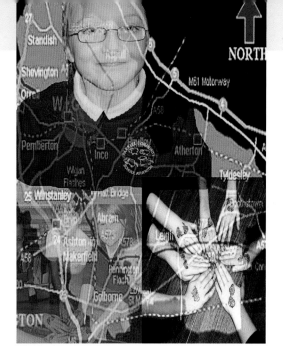

Gather pupils around the interactive whiteboard and demonstrate how to open a new A4 page on which to create their collage. Start by opening a map image and show them how to cut out a section and move it to the new blank page. Scale the map to cover the whole of the new A4 page (to refer back to the method, see the *Photoshop Elements*: **Selection tools and layers Masterclass** in *Art Express* Books 3 and 4). Instruct pupils to do the same and then save the image.

■ Call the class together and show how to apply additional layers over the map. Ask the children to open an image of themselves, cut out a section and drag this to the map image. Ask them to repeat the process adding images of friends, family and a favourite object. Save the image.

■ Now demonstrate to the class how to review their layers. Remind them how to select each layer in the Layer palette and how to scale and adjust the opacity of each layer to create a merged self-image. Encourage pupils to experiment with filter effects on some of the layers, saving several versions of the image.

■ Initiate a debate with the group about the various images they have created and then ask them to work in pairs as 'critical friends' to discuss and review which image best represents the idea of themselves. Ensure that every child has a chance to speak.

■ Finally, ask the children to choose two different images each for printing. They will use these to make the collage in Session 2.

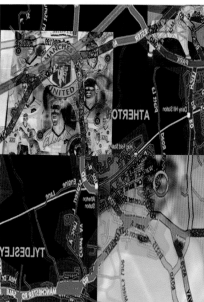

DIFFERENTIATION

Children who have not progressed as far...
Some pupils may need additional help in choosing sections from their images. Pair the children sensitively to support each other in selecting and manipulating their images.

Children who have progressed further...
These pupils could make further adjustments to their image by applying filters in selected areas and experimenting with different colour combinations. They could also be challenged to make additional images, selecting photographs from other children to be used on the support for the structure.

SESSION 2 **MAKING AND COMPLETING THE STRUCTURE**

LEARNING OBJECTIVES
Children will:
- learn to prepare their structure and plan purposefully how to achieve their creative idea
- learn to use and apply new techniques and explore their possibilities
- learn to explain and evaluate their own work in relation to the work of their classmates, and be able to suggest refinements.

VOCABULARY **collage, transfer**

▼ RESOURCES

- ▸ computer printouts or transfers
- ▸ wood and sandpaper
- ▸ white acrylic or emulsion paint
- ▸ PVA glue
- ▸ hooks and eyes
- ▸ resource sheets: Making the structure; Using Lazertran (1–4)

▼ ASSESSMENT FOR LEARNING

Can the children:
- ▸ prepare the materials for their collage?
- ▸ apply their image using collage or transfer?
- ▸ describe the process and discuss how the individual works look together?

ACTIVITY

Prior to this session, prepare several pieces of 5cm x 2.5cm timber to make the backing structure (see the **Making the structure** resource sheet). Computer images can be printed on different types of paper or transfer and applied to different surfaces. This project used Lazertran as the transfer paper; the process could be carried out using computer printouts. (See the **Using Lazertran** resource sheets.)

■ Talk to the children about the methods they are going to use in order to create their self-portrait structure. Explain that they will apply their images to the wood using a mixture of collage and Lazertran and that, when completed, their individual pieces will hang together on the class wall to make a group portrait.

■ First, pupils need to sand their strip of wood. Demonstrate how to sand the surface to remove loose splinters and smooth edges. Once completed, brush the wood with white paint, leaving some of the area exposed – this will add variation to the surface once the images are applied.

■ Call the children together and describe how to tear parts of their collage to stick onto the wood using watered-down PVA (see the **Using Lazertran** resource sheets). Remind them to tear the design carefully to show the different parts of their self-image. Repeat the process to complete the collage and assemble according to the instructions.

■ Ask the class to reflect on their work with a talking partner, suggesting any areas they found more challenging or would like to improve on. Then group together for a discussion about the completed structure.

■ If time allows, pupils could make two end products – one to take home and another to leave in school as a semi-permanent display about the members of that year group.

DIFFERENTIATION

Children who have not progressed as far...
These pupils may need additional assistance with tearing their printouts for their collage. It might be helpful to use a black and white version of their image to practise tearing. The children could also work in pairs to support each other.

Children who have progressed further...
Suggest that these pupils use their additional images to create the support for the structures. They can also be paired with other children to assist them in tearing and applying their collage to the wood.

SESSION 3 VICTORIAN PAPER COSTUMES

LEARNING OBJECTIVES
Children will:

- learn to work collaboratively by working in groups to create a paper costume on a theme
- learn to experiment with new techniques by using paper construction
- learn how art can be used to evoke emotions and feelings by considering how to reflect their ideas about child labour in their work.

VOCABULARY Victorian, testimony, collaborative, character

ACTIVITY

This project was developed as part of a cross-curricular art and history project on mining and child labour in Victorian times. Pupils looked at children's testimonies and discussed what it would have been like to endure similar working conditions. They researched the jobs and clothing, and then developed character stories in preparation for a creative composition about life down the mine.

Prior to the session in your class, print some images that the children can use for reference. The session can be translated into any appropriate time and culture.

- Explain to the class that they will create a paper costume based on Victorian children's clothing. The finished costume will be used for a character story and modified using *Photoshop Elements*.
- Show some images of Victorian children's clothing (see the CD-ROM) and discuss the components.
- Demonstrate how to construct a basic costume using newsprint

(see the **Costume construction techniques** resource sheet). Provide groups of four or five pupils with a reference image and ask them to use the construction techniques as a starting point for their costume. The purpose is to encourage pupils to think creatively, talk and respond immediately using the newspaper, and not spend hours on the design.

- Ask the children to work as a team to decide who is making each part of the costume and to select a model (for example, two people make the body of the costume, one makes the hat, others make straps or belts).
- Once complete, photograph the model from different viewpoints, preferably against a green screen (see the relevant resource sheet from *Art Express* Book 3).
- At the end of the session, discuss the finished costumes, including their suitability for the purpose. This will help the children to concentrate on the 'characters' for the costumes, prior to Session 4.

▼ RESOURCES

- ▶ A4 paper
- ▶ newspapers, newsprint or white crepe paper
- ▶ masking tape
- ▶ glue sticks
- ▶ scissors
- ▶ CD-ROM: images of Victorian costume
- ▶ resource sheet: Costume construction techniques

▼ ASSESSMENT FOR LEARNING

Can the children:
- ▶ work collaboratively to make their costume?
- ▶ resolve problems and develop control of the media?
- ▶ use images effectively to reflect their ideas and emotions?

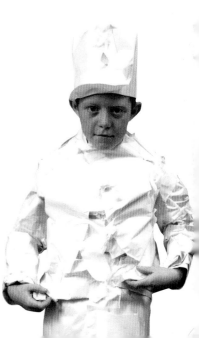

DIFFERENTIATION

Children who have not progressed as far...
Pupils can be grouped carefully so that less confident children can be supported by the group. These individuals may need support to identify basic construction methods.

Children who have progressed further...
Challenge these pupils to invent different ways to use paper construction to add decorative effects to their costumes. Encourage them to experiment on a smaller scale to test construction techniques. Invite high-performing groups to identify and delegate specific tasks, producing a streamlined production line.

SESSION 4 **CHARACTER STORIES AND COSTUMES**

LEARNING OBJECTIVES
Children will:

- refine their knowledge and skills using digital media

- learn to use their imagination to select and plan by researching and combining images and text to create their composition
- learn that creative ideas can be developed in response to different stimuli.

VOCABULARY **illustrate, layer, testimony**

▼ RESOURCES

- ▶ photographs of costumes from Session 3
- ▶ computer
- ▶ image-manipulation software with layers (for example, *Photoshop Elements*)
- ▶ printer
- ▶ Presentation: *Photoshop Elements:* Text and page layout Masterclass
- ▶ CD-ROM: demonstration costume image

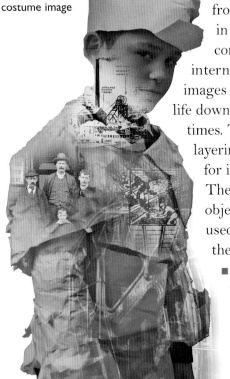

ACTIVITY

Prior to this session, pupils will need to discuss again what it would have been like to endure working conditions in a Victorian mine. They should look again at the children's testimonies and work in groups to develop ideas prior to writing their own short testimony of life down the mines. The stories need to be typed using *Microsoft Word* and saved for use in Session 5.

- In preparation for this session, download the costume images from Session 3 and put them in a shared area on the computer network. Use the internet to search for and collect images and illustrations showing life down the mines in Victorian times. These will be used for layering onto the costumes and for inclusion in the final layout. The selection might feature objects or tools that can be used to illustrate the story.
  - On the interactive whiteboard, show pupils the demonstration costume image (see the CD-ROM).

Talk to the children about the demonstration image, and show them the individual layers that make up the costume design. Explain that they will illustrate the costume with different images but that they need to prepare their costume image first.

- Show pupils how to open one of their costume images from Session 3. Explain that they will remove all the

! USEFUL WEBSITES

For information about working in Victorian mines and examples of children's testimonies, see:
- www.learningcurve.gov.uk/victorianbritain/industrial/default.htm
- www.victorianweb.org/history/ashley.html

background information around the costume. This is the same as the process used in *Art Express* Books 3, 4 and 5 and is easier if the costumes have been photographed against a green screen. Demonstrate how to use the Magic Wand in *Photoshop Elements* to remove the green background (refer to the **Green screen** resource sheet in *Art Express* Book 3). When all of the background information has been removed, save the image using a new name.

■ Talk to the class about layering Victorian mining images over the paper costume so that the costume shows aspects of life down the mines in Victorian times. Open up the demonstration image and show pupils how the costume has been layered. Open one of the children's images and one of the mining images. Use the Lasso tool to cut out a section from the mining images and paste it onto the costume image. Use the Opacity slider or Overlay option to merge the image with the costume. Request the class to do the same, then save the image.

■ Repeat the process several times until the costume is covered with different mining images. Continue to save as necessary as new images are added.

■ When pupils have layered their costume image, call them together at the interactive whiteboard. Explain that they are going to review their layers before merging them to create a single image. Show them the demonstration image again and ask them to look at each layer in turn and to check the transparency, so that the costume can be seen below the layer. Explain that before using their image in the story, they should join all the layers together to make a single image.

■ Demonstrate how to flatten the image in the Layer palette. Save the image using a new name. (For more on this, see the *Photoshop Elements*: **Text and page layout** Masterclass.)

DIFFERENTIATION

Children who have not progressed as far...
Some pupils will need additional help with layering their costume. Pair the children carefully to support each other. In a plenary session, groups that have been particularly successful can be invited to explain their process so that others can learn.

Children who have progressed further...
These pupils could share each other's images to create a second character costume to be used in their final design. They can be invited to share their ideas and thinking with the whole class.

SESSION 5 **CREATING THE CHARACTER STORY**

LEARNING OBJECTIVES

Children will:

■ learn to be open-minded and recognise that, in art, meaning can be communicated by combining different elements

■ reaffirm the need for clarity of purpose and planning when designing

■ learn to review and evaluate their work and their working process.

Rose Edwards

My name is Rose Edwards I am 10 and work at the local mine wich is wet, dark and dusty. It is a snoby rich person named Mr E Jhonson.

I work there as a putter I have broke everyone o, toes as I am very weak and the coal is so heavy I always drop it. One time my freind [a puller] le a cart and as it came down it took off one of my a Minning is a nightmare. A mine is the worst pla. EVER

By the end of my shift I have nearly coughed m out! The only reason I still work here is because t

VOCABULARY illustrate, layout, combine, design template, style elements

▼ **RESOURCES**

▶ children's own short, imagined testimonies of life down the mines
▶ computer
▶ image-manipulation software with layers (for example, *Photoshop Elements*)
▶ printer
▶ CD-ROM: sample design template
▶ resource sheet: Page layout
▶ pupil self-evaluation sheet

ACTIVITY

This session brings together the work done in Sessions 3 and 4, along with the children's stories, to create an illustrated design. In preparation for this session, you will need to consider design and layout.

A good example of the type of layout you are aiming for is shown in Dorling Kindersley's *Eyewitness Guides*. On their website (www.dorlingkindersley-uk.co.uk), you can view page layouts that combine text and image to tell a story on a theme.

Alternatively, you could assemble a collection of highly illustrated books of the pupils' choice.

■ Provide a range of *Eyewitness Guides* (or similar) for the children to look at. Ask them to work in pairs to consider the arrangement of text and images on the pages. Talk to them about page

layout and how it is a part of graphic design that deals with arrangements and style of elements on a page. Reveal that designers often use a design template to give a consistent look to the pages of a book.

■ On the interactive whiteboard, show the class one of the page layouts from the Dorling Kindersley website. Talk to them about the style of the page and the use of columns (display the examples on the **Page layout** resource sheet). Discuss also the balance of shapes, blocks of text, images, headings and captions.

Give the children copies of the sample design template (print these out from the CD-ROM), and ask them to make some preliminary sketches using pencil and paper to consider the layout of their own page. Encourage pupils to try out two or three ideas in rough before starting work on the computer. This will give them a better idea of the scale of the images and will help them plan where to position the text in relation to the images.

■ Using the interactive whiteboard, demonstrate how to open the sample design template (see the CD-ROM). Explain that the lines on the page are guidelines and will not appear in the final image.

■ Show how to open the costume image and cut and paste it onto the design template. By now, the children

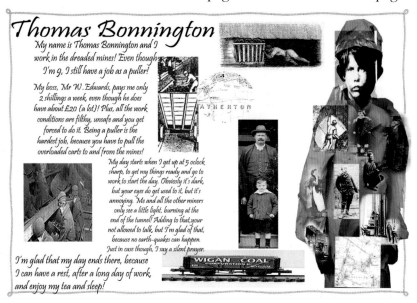

Thomas Bonnington

My name is Thomas Bonnington and I work in the dreaded mines! Even though I'm 9, I still have a job as a puller!

My boss, Mr W. Edwards, pays me only 2 shillings a week, even though he does have about £20 (a lot)! Plus, all the work conditions are filthy, unsafe and you get forced to do it. Being a puller is the hardest job, because you have to pull the overloaded carts to and from the mines!

My day starts when I get up at 5 oclock sharp, to get my things ready and go to work to start the day. Obviously it's dark, but your eyes do get used to it, but it's annoying. Me and all the other miners only see a little light, burning at the end of the tunnel! Adding to that, your not allowed to talk, but I'm glad of that, because no earth-quakes can happen. Just in case though, I say a silent prayer.

I'm glad that my day ends there, because I can have a rest, after a long day of work, and enjoy my tea and sleep!

should be familiar with cutting and pasting between images. Ask them to do the same and position their costume image on the page. Save the image.

■ Open your *Word* document and demonstrate how to copy the story text and paste it onto the page (see the ***Photoshop Elements*: Text and page layout** Masterclass). Ask pupils to repeat the process, pasting in their mining images to add detail to their story. Lastly, they can add headings and captions as necessary.

■ Show the children how to review their image, edit their layers, and adjust the size and position of the different elements to create a balanced composition.

■ Now split the class into groups to discuss the project. Encourage them to assess their work against the learning objectives, and reflect on how they overcame any challenges the unit presented, and how they would like to use their new skills in the future. You could also provide each child with the **Pupil self-evaluation** sheet, to be filled in at school or at home.

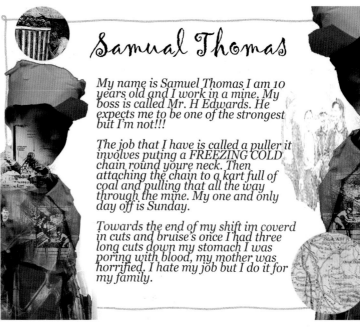

Samual Thomas

My name is Samuel Thomas I am 10 years old and I work in a mine. My boss is called Mr H Edwards. He expects me to be one of the strongest but I'm not!!!

The job that I have is called a puller it involves puting a FREEZING COLD chain round youre neck. Then attaching the chain to a kart full of coal and pulling that all the way through the mine. My one and only day off is Sunday.

Towards the end of my shift im coverd in cuts and bruise's once I had three long cuts down my stomach I was poring with blood, my mother was horrified. I hate my job but I do it for my family.

VARIATIONS

The ideas from this session could be adapted to combine with the work done in Sessions 1 and 2. Children could make a double-page feature in the style of a Dorling Kindersley book about their time at the school. Combine one feature from every child to form a yearbook to mark the end of their time at primary school.

▼ ASSESSMENT FOR LEARNING

Can the children:
▸ combine selected elements to create an illustrated story?
▸ create a clear, uncluttered layout?
▸ review and modify their work appropriately?

Thomas Bonnington

My name is Thomas Bonnington, I am 9 years old and I work at the local mine in Atherton. The mine is owned by Mr E. Smith He is a firm but fair foreman.

Before i'm set for work I get a cold bottle of tea for breakfast. When I arrive at work I tell Mr E. Smith I am there and then start my shift. My shift is 12 hours long. My job is called a puller. I have to get a metal strap, tie it around me and attach it to the cart then pull it to the top. The cart and the coal as you can imagine is very heavy and that is why I have a bad back in the morning.

At lunch I get my tatty ,tinned lunchbox out and have my sandwiches as well as the rest of my cold tea.

Under the mine it is very dark and hot, your eyes adjust to the dark and because it is hot you start to sweat. Even though it is boring it is well worth doing it for the money. I get 2 shillings everyday . That helps us buy my family food and keep us under a roof.

This is a picture a boy in 1887 !

! HANDY HINT

Pupils should organise all their information into a single folder on the computer. This should include their costume image, their story as a *Word* document, and the additional mining images they plan to use to illustrate their page.

Having all the resources in one place eliminates the need to search in different folders for the images.

DIFFERENTIATION

Children who have not progressed as far...
Some pupils will need additional support in composing their picture. Pair the children carefully to assist each other.

Children who have progressed further...
These pupils can use additional characters and images to illustrate their story or to experiment with different layouts.

OTHER AREAS OF LEARNING

GEOGRAPHY
- Set a competition for pupils to exploit a range of digital processes to explore ways of improving the look of the school and local environments – the best design or presentation wins.

LITERACY
- Digital collage can be used to develop fantasy images based on poems or stories.
- Explore book-cover illustration and ask pupils to work together to design a cover for a well-known book, combining drawings, photographs and text.

Digital media

HISTORY
- Pupils can create digital images locating themselves in different historical scenes.
- Children could explore what it was like to live in the past by taking photographs of local buildings and comparing them to archive images of the same buildings. They could then write stories of what it would have been like to live or work there and layer text over the images.

PHYSICAL, SOCIAL AND HEALTH EDUCATION (PSHE)
- Pupils could create a digital collage using images from newspapers to comment on a recent local, national or international event.

ICT
- Children can use digital processes to combine drawn, scanned and photographic images to create a multimedia presentation based on the local environment or a local event.

ART AND DESIGN
- Digital media can be used to extend a range of ideas developed using traditional media.
- Develop the children's sense of place – ask them to take photographs of the local environment and layer different elements to create a collage that makes a statement about the local area.